"That's Not Odd ... That's GOD!"

Recognizing His Presence; Rejoicing in His Providence

David Stanford

WESTBOW
PRESS
A DIVISION OF THOMAS NELSON
& ZONDERVAN

WestBow Press books may be ordered through booksellers or by contacting:

WestBow Press
A Division of Thomas Nelson
1663 Liberty Drive
Bloomington, IN 47403
www.westbowpress.com
1 (866) 928-1240

Because of the dynamic nature of the Internet, any web addresses or links contained in this book may have changed since publication and may no longer be valid. The views expressed in this work are solely those of the author and do not necessarily reflect the views of the publisher, and the publisher hereby disclaims any responsibility for them.

Any people depicted in stock imagery provided by Thinkstock are models, and such images are being used for illustrative purposes only. Certain stock imagery © Thinkstock.

ISBN: 978-1-4908-1423-0 (sc)
ISBN: 978-1-4908-1422-3 (e)

Library of Congress Control Number: 2013919644

Printed in the United States of America.

WestBow Press rev. date: 4/25/2013

Contents

TO DEBBIE

This book does not contain my stories; it contains our stories. Not only are you an integral part of all this book entails, you are a very real part of me, and I, of you. As we have parented together, served the Lord together, adventured together, and grown together, life has become a series of stories I will always treasure. Your heart for the Lord is pure and steadfast. Your love and faithfulness to me, keep me going. I can't wait to see what lies ahead, as we continue our journey into the future. I will always love you, and will always thank our Lord for letting you and me become partners together, in this exciting earthly sojourn called life.

TO DAD AND MOM

Although many things in my life have changed over the years, your love and encouragement to me, have been constant. Never have I doubted your love; and never have I lacked your support. Thank you for modeling these important qualities for me, every moment of my life. Thank you, that for as long as I can remember, you have demonstrated what it means to faithfully walk with the Lord. I love you, so much, and thank you for always being there for me.

THAT'S NOT ODD...THAT'S GOD!

Overview

When all hope is gone; when the funds are depleted; when time has run out; when facing the impossible; when there's *just no way*...these are the very times God loves to intersect our lives and display His all-sufficient wisdom and power. In his book, "That's not odd...That's God!", David Stanford invites you to accompany him and his wife, Debbie, on a hope-filled journey, encompassing thirty-plus years of pastoral ministry. This journey includes ten specific stops, where God directly intersected His life, often in very unexpected ways. Be ready to laugh, cry, and be in awe, at the ways God reveals His Person, and demonstrates His provision. But this is not just a book about the Stanfords; it is a ten-part tribute to the knowledge, power, and compassion, God loves to demonstrate in the lives of each of His children. When God decides to show up, in ways only He can, the experience is life-changing and unforgettable. From "No Way!"... to "Yes, way!"... to "Yaweh!", let the stories in this book encourage you to take a closer look at the ongoing work of God, behind the scenes, in your life. Then move forward with the courage and confidence which rises, when pausing to recognize His unseen hand. You too, will want to join David and Debbie in joyfully proclaiming, "No, That's not odd...That's GOD!"

THAT'S NOT ODD...THAT'S GOD!

Hello, I'm David, and I've got problems. You see, my wife, Debbie, and I, are about as human as you can get. And during our more than one-third century of shared life and ministry, we have had our portion of difficulties, disappointments, doubts, and discouragements. At times we have blown it royally, and suffered the corresponding consequences. Other times we've inadvertently made costly mistakes or poor choices, teaching us tough, but important, life-lessons. Our problems, whether self-inflicted or not, have been the soil from which faith has sprung, as we have learned, and continue learning to depend on God for needed answers. I once heard someone say, "If you desire to have faith, you're asking for problems; because for faith to be effective, it must have some place to work." Faith is active, not passive, and therefore has to have a reason to be deployed. Needs beget faith; problems encourage faith; difficulties cultivate faith. Life's struggles are the soil in which true faith can grow. I love the old Gospel song entitled "Through It All", authored by Gloria Gaither. A part of one verse expresses it well:

> *"If I'd never had a problem,*
> *I wouldn't know that God could solve 'em;*
> *I wouldn't know what faith in God can do".*

God knows, and He cares...

Therefore, a great portion of our life-story, or stories, has to do with God's providential care, in response to our cries for help. Some of these times of Divine deliverance have been nothing short of miraculous. At times we've seen huge pressing needs met unexpectedly, problems solved unexplainably, and deliverance from difficulties occur unconventionally. These experiences have served to renew our courage and strength; often when it seemed all hope was gone. At times, we have found ourselves weeping tears of pure, unabated joy; while at other times, our response was one of reverential awe and wonder. Still other occasions left us holding our sides with convulsions of hysterical belly-laughter. But in each of these situations, it was supremely evident that we had experienced the personal touch of God, in our very own everyday lives. He had singled us out; He had visited us; He had acted on our behalf. These moments of Divine intervention have resulted in the undeniable awareness that He knows who we are, where we live, and what we need at any given time or situation.

We're all in the same boat...

But Debbie and I also know we aren't the only ones who understand what difficulties are all about. Hardly a day goes by, in which we don't hear of someone desperately needing God's touch in their lives. Almost every family I know, has "issues" of some variety. All of us will become intimately familiar with heartache, need, and pain along life's journey. Just pick up a newspaper, turn on the daily news, listen to the talk at the gym....or look in the mirror. Yes, problems come to us all. It happens to be a very real part of the human experience. This fact is one of the most often repeated themes in the Bible.

In the oldest book of the Bible, the human author, Job, penned these words, _"Man who is born of a woman is few of days and full of trouble."_ (ESV) Centuries later, Jesus Christ Himself said these words to his followers, _"In this godless world you will continue to experience difficulties."_ (The Message). Put these two statements together, paraphrase them, and here's what you have: _"Everyone who lives on planet earth, and whose mother was a woman, can expect to have problems."_ (author's paraphrase) Dear reader, holding this book, I may not know much about you. Our lives may not have intersected yet, but I can say with some authority, that unless you are an alien from outer space, this includes YOU. And guess what? You're not alone. Actually, you're in pretty good company.

Our purpose(s)

Therefore, the purpose of this book is really three-fold. First, a desire to share what God has done in the lives of Debbie and me, in hopes that our experiences will serve to encourage others along the way. I want those currently going through a tough stretch of road, or a rough season of life, to realize God is able and sufficient to meet any and every need. I also have a soft place in my heart for fellow-ministers, and hope the examples of God's sufficiency during our many years of ministry, will bolster them in their battle. Perhaps you don't fit either of these categories, but you simply need a booster-shot of faith. God's providence to Debbie and me has certainly bolstered ours, so our prayer is that these stories will give you a faith-lift as well. In it all, and through it all, my ultimate desire is that God receives the glory for the ways He has continually proven His compassionate care to us.

Why the strange title?

Throughout the years, as we have verbally related some of these personal experiences to others, very often the response would come in the form of an astonished, "Wow… that certainly is odd." In many of these conversations, I often found myself instinctively shooting back, "No, actually, that's not odd… that's just God."

So, looking back over the past three decades, I've reached the conclusion that God's hand and/or handiwork is evidently woven throughout our "story". As a matter of fact, He *is* our story. There is no other way to explain much of what has been observed and experienced, as we've simply tried to minister to, and for Him, along life's pathway. I am fully aware that many of the things, which make up "our story", are the same kinds of things other people experience. But as they are viewed in the context of God's gracious providence, the miraculous comes into focus. He thrills to "show up" along the sojourn of life – often when least expected. Just ask the two Disciples who had a startling, personal encounter with the resurrected Christ, while walking the Emmaus Road. You can find the details of their story in Luke's account of the Gospel. (24:13-35).

Therefore, this is not a unique or special story, nor is it a new one; but it happens to be *our* story…or stories. Thank you for allowing me to share some of them with you. And when God makes Himself clearly evident in **your** life situations, our prayer is that you won't think it odd; but rather, in jaw dropping awe and wonder, joyful ecstasy, or even gales of uncontrollable laughter, recognize it as the hand of a personal, caring, all-sufficient God. Then in those moments, you too can say, "No, that's not odd….that's God!"

Putting A Handle On It

I must share one more thing, before we get started. Years ago, while leading and shepherding a group of faithful Sunday School workers, I often reminded them they shouldn't teach the Bible as if giving a lecture, or making a presentation. Rather, they should strive to keep it interesting, engage the students, and always, always, *always* "put a handle on it". I told them it is hard to carry a basket-full of something, if the basket has no handle to hold, nothing to grip. So, at the end of each lesson, after dispensing Bible knowledge, sharing Scriptural facts, etc., a good teacher concludes by putting a handle on it. The "handle" allows the students to carry the living truths of God's Word with them, and apply them to life situations throughout the coming week or month. The "handle" helps the listener personalize what they have heard or read; releasing Biblical truth and principles to become active and relevant in their lives. The Apostle Paul, who is credited for writing nearly half the New Testament, told his Philippian followers, "*Those things, which you have both learned, and received, and heard, and seen in me, **do**: and the God of peace shall be with you.*" (KJV Philippians 4:9, emphasis mine).

Therefore, at the end of each chapter in this book, you will find a section called, "Putting A Handle On It". I sincerely ask that this section not be overlooked, or skipped. Instead, please use it to enhance application of the principles discovered in these stories. My prayer is that the things which have shaped the lives of Debbie and me, will have a lasting impact on you... as well as on those God allows you to influence for His kingdom. My desire is to place some things in the basket of your life, which you can carry off and use; hold and examine; or take out and share - long after you lay this book down.

Please understand these chapters are not intended just to be stories which entertain; or even inspire. No, no, a thousand times no! I certainly hope they will encourage and inspire, but these are stories, deliberately shared, with the purposeful intent to add hope, where it may have diminished. They are meant to bolster courage and evoke confidence to push ahead, in the face of difficult, if not impossible circumstances. They are conveyed with the desire to embolden the heart of each reader, with the life changing knowledge that our God truly is present... aware... able... active... compassionate... sufficient. In the same way the two Emmaus disciples hurried back to Jerusalem, to share with their friends, the things they had experienced (Luke 24); in that very same way, I desire to speak into your heart our experiences, and the corresponding Biblical truths. His involvement in our lives are not coincidence, nor are they odd...they're simply and succinctly...God. Recognize Him. Believe Him. Embrace Him. Trust Him. Love Him. Enjoy Him. Obey Him. Share Him. And above all, be sure you do not fail to acknowledge Him. For you never know how, or when, or where, He might decide to reveal Himself in your own story -- which in reality, is simply another beautiful chapter of His-story.

Chapter One

FIRED, BUT NOT FINISHED!

(Philippians 1:6; Hebrews 10:35)

Iron sharpens iron

Buddy McCord has long been one of my mentors, probably without even knowing it. I've observed him admiringly, from a distance, as he faithfully and fruitfully served the Lord for many, many years. And even though he only is a few years my senior, any time I have been privileged to spend time with him, my life has been noticeably enhanced. My earliest memory of rubbing shoulders with Bud, took place during my first full-time job in the ministry. I was a fresh-out-of-Bible-College pastoral staff member at the Thomas Road Baptist Church, in Lynchburg, VA. My ministry duties were divided between the church and Liberty University. When we arrived on the scene, Buddy and his sweet wife, Pam, had already been serving there for several years. But they were making preparations to move to Brazil, where they would continue their ministry.

My job entailed a number of things, including the leadership of a college student ministry team, called S.M.I.T.E. (Student Missionary Intern Training for Evangelism). As I busied myself learning the ropes, it gave Bud and me several months, to work together. During those days, as our ministry lives overlapped, I tried to take advantage of each opportunity to spend time with my mentor. I was often impressed with the great wisdom, and Spiritual insight he had, for such a young man. On one occasion as were "solving the world's problems" over lunch, he shared a truth with me, which neither of us realized, would one day have a major impact on my life.

1

During the conversation that day, we found ourselves discussing the importance of understanding "God's Will" in a given situation. The statement he made to me went something like this: "Before you set out to do a certain thing, make positively sure, without a shadow of a doubt, it is the will of God for your life. No matter what it takes, nail it down completely. That way, when difficulties come - and they always do - you won't succumb to the pressure to quit. Because if you know for sure, that you are doing God's will, that knowledge gives you staying power, through the storms you will face." I mentally catalogued that bit of wisdom, and went on about my business. Little did I know how that conversation would play out in my life, further down the road.

Fast-forward nearly six years. Deb and I had been tossed about by some pretty severe personal storms after leaving Lynchburg. Furthermore, we and found ourselves out of "vocational ministry", and living in the Washington D.C. area, where I worked three jobs, just to keep our growing family afloat. My primary day-job was with a major HVAC company, working as the warehouse and parts manager. Not only was it back-breaking work, but there were nearly 100 employees in our branch, with only me, and one secretary, claiming to be followers of Christ. The guys in the shop were a pretty crusty and profane bunch, who seemed to enjoy riding me constantly, about my faith. On top of that I had two other side jobs, plus several weekly responsibilities at our church. I stayed exhausted – physically, emotionally and spiritually. Debbie and I found ourselves crying out to the Lord to please open the door for us to re-enter the ministry, which I knew was my life's calling, and true heart's desire.

Focused Prayer

Because we knew we would probably need to re-locate, when/if a ministry position came open, we began to discuss where we would choose to go, were the choice left up to us. After thinking about it and discussing it for awhile, we agreed that our number one choice would be the Florence Baptist Temple, in Florence, SC, where Dr. William T. (Bill) Monroe was the founder and senior pastor. At that time, the church had approximately 3000 members, along with a fully accredited Christian school. We had visited the church a few years earlier, and fell in love with it. Plus, the pastor had greatly impressed me, several years earlier, when he spoke in chapel while I was a Bible college student.

We decided to make it a matter of focused prayer, and not to mention it to anyone outside of our family. We told our very young children, Nathan – 7; Natalie – 4; and Emily 1 ½ that we were going to ask God to let us move to Florence, so Daddy could work in the church. The girls were too young to fully understand, but all three children joined us in praying, with the faith that often puts us adults to shame - simply asking, and believing, that God would answer. I still remember listening to Nathan and Natalie, praying "Dear God, would You let us go to Florence?" Deb and I also prayed very specifically that this would be the place, where God would open the door and allow me to re-enter the ministry I loved. We were living approximately eight hours from Florence at the time, and had no idea if the church even had an opening, or needed additional staff. We only knew that it was where we desired to be, and had covenanted together in prayer that God would work out the details – in His way, and in His time…just as long as it was soon!

Adding fuel to the fire

After this had been going on for a couple of months, I was hard at work one day when I received a message to come to the office, for an important phone call. Debbie was phoning to tell me she had received a call from one of my former college buddies, who happened to be serving on the pastoral staff of the Florence Baptist Temple. (It had been years since I last heard from him.) He left a message with Deb, asking me call him back as soon as possible. Obviously my curiosity was piqued, so I returned the call at the first opportunity. He told me Pastor Monroe had him contact me, to find out if I could come there to visit Florence Baptist Temple for the weekend. I asked him why I was being invited to come, to which he replied, he didn't know, he was just told to convey the message. Hmmm.

The upcoming weekend was Labor Day weekend, a long weekend for me, so it was a perfect time to make the trip to Florence. I told him we'd be there. Then I hung up and called Deb, instructing her to get busy packing. We would be spending the weekend in Florence!

Taking Friday off from work, so we could travel, gave us Saturday and Sunday, to be available for whatever Pastor Monroe had in mind. After letting him know we were in town, he said he wanted to meet with me the next morning in his office. We arrived, early and excited, and talked together for a couple of hours. The conversation covered all kinds of things - where Deb and I had been the past few years, what we had experienced, and what we hoped to see happen in the future, etc. I did not mention we had been praying specifically to be able to come to Florence; but I did tell him it was my desire to be back in a full-time ministry position, as a church staff member. We left the meeting extremely encouraged, and eagerly anticipating the next day's worship service.

A wonderful weekend

We felt like special guests as we enjoyed being a part of FBT that Sunday. The inspiring music, the powerful preaching of God's Word, and the encouraging atmosphere were strongly evident in this great church - so abundantly blessed of the Lord. Our months of prayer, and desire to be a part of this ministry were only intensified by the experiences of the day. After church we were treated to lunch by Pastor and Mrs. Monroe, where we talked more about ministry-related topics. Following lunch, we were taken back to our car, where we said our goodbyes. Pastor Monroe (affectionately called "Preacher" by many of his staff and church members) made no commitment to us, but did indicate that he was planning to add someone to the church staff in the near future. I felt that our time together had gone very well. All the way back to Virginia we talked excitedly about the wonderful weekend we had experienced. It had been such a breath of fresh air to be there, and we longed for more of the same.

Once back home, we jumped right back into our stressful routine, and awaited the phone call asking us to move to Florence. We also continued to pray with renewed intensity. But pray as we might, the call did not come. We had left Florence feeling very positive about the future, but as we continued to pray about it, nothing seemed to be happening. We tried to remain hopeful, while fighting the growing feelings of disappointment and discouragement.

Putting feet to our prayers

September turned to October, and our hope continued to fade. Then, about one week into November, while I was at work, Debbie was listening to a radio program which really got her attention. In it, the speaker exhorted the listeners to step out and pro-actively live by faith, rather than passively sit by, hoping something will happen. When I came home from work later that day, I couldn't believe my eyes. Our small apartment was stripped bare. She had taken down all the pictures from the walls, and had begun packing all of our things in boxes, which were lining the hallway, from one end to the other.

"Daddy, we're moving to Flowence!", an excited Natalie met me at the door (she cutely pronounced her Rs like Ws back then).

"Really? Who said so?"

"Mommy told me."

"Is that right???"

"Honey, why didn't you tell me Pastor Monroe called?", I asked, excited but somewhat confused.

"Well… actually… he hasn't called" she said, rather sheepishly. "I just decided that we needed to 'put feet to the prayer we've been praying', so I started packing up our things…. sort of by faith."

I couldn't argue with her faith, or her willingness to put it to action, so we lived out of boxes for the next few weeks, still waiting for the call we just knew would come any day. During those weeks, I couldn't find socks, a coffee cup, or anything else, without digging through boxes. I tried not to complain, but wondered how long this would go on.

God's sense of humor

The week before Thanksgiving, Debbie either had a lapse of faith, got bored, or became tired of searching through boxes. So in the same way she had packed it all up in one day, she decided to put it all back where it came from. Every last bit of it. (Now I know this next part will sound like a gross exaggeration, but I promise it happened *exactly* the way I'm about to relate it. Honest to goodness!)

Having just finished unpacking all the boxes, and putting all of our earthly belongings back away, Debbie found herself standing on one of our kitchen chairs, hammering the very last nail in the very last wall-hanging, when the phone rang.

"Will you go answer that, Nathan?", she asked as she stepped back to see if the picture was perfectly straight.

Nathan answered in his most courteous manner, as he had been taught, then laid the phone down, and ran into the living room to get his Mom. (This was when phones still had cords attached to them. And yes, we're *that* old.)

"Who is it, Nathan?" she asked, while intently studying at the freshly hung picture.

"It's Pastor Monroe", he stated, matter-of-factly.

Debbie nearly fainted on the spot. She had stubbornly held out by faith for three weeks, and the *very moment* she reversed her faith decision, the long-awaited call came.

She nervously picked up the phone.

"Debbie, this is Pastor Monroe, from Florence. I was wondering if you and David could come back and visit with us again this weekend. I know it is short notice, but I'd really like you to come, if you can arrange to do it."

"Why thank you, Pastor. I'll call David right away and see what he says. But I'm sure we can work it out."

On the road again

I came home to a perfectly straightened apartment, and a very embarrassed wife. The following weekend was Thanksgiving, and we had already made plans to visit my parents in Savannah, GA, which is located approximately two and a half hours from Florence. So, following the Thanksgiving observance with my family, it worked out perfectly, to leave the kids with Mom and Dad, as Deb and I made a second trip to Florence for Saturday and Sunday. We were nearly ecstatic about the job offer we knew finally awaited us there.

The weekend in Florence was "déjà vu" of the previous visit: Saturday meeting in the office; encouraging time of worship on Sunday; lunch afterwards with the Pastor and Norma; being dropped off at my car, with thank yous and good-byes kindly exchanged. Suddenly I felt panic-stricken. I sensed our opportunity slipping away, and couldn't believe what was happening… nor could I let it end this way again.

"Excuse me, Pastor Monroe!", I hurriedly waved him down, as he was about drive away.

"Yes David? Did you forget something?"

"Well no, but…" I was searching for the right words. "This is our second trip down here from Virginia, and we've thoroughly enjoyed both occasions, but I'm still not sure where we stand with you. Could you please let me know what you're thinking, with regards to your staff situation, before we leave?"

He paused briefly, before answering.

"Well, do you think you would like to be a part of our pastoral staff?", he asked, very pointedly.

"Why y-y-yes, I think we would", I replied, trying to act coy, as my insides were on the verge of exploding.

"Ok, then I'll be looking for you the first of January", he stated. And just like that, he sped out of the parking lot, leaving me standing there with my face hanging out.

"Honey, I hoped you saved the boxes."

Florence, at last!

January could not arrive soon enough. We were so excited, not only about the opportunity to enter the ministry again, but the privilege of doing so in such a great place. And most of all, we were thrilled God had graciously honored our prayer of faith, as we had prayed so very specifically for Him to allow us to be a part of the ministry team at FBT. For the rest of my life, I would never again be able to doubt God answers prayer. And I cannot adequately express, the great degree to which this bolstered my prayer life.

Rough sailing

However, joining the staff at FBT was as intimidating as it was exciting. Although the other staff members were very kind and accommodating, most of them had been working together, in that place, for nearly 10 years. Under Pastor Monroe's capable leadership, the ministry ran like a well-oiled machine, with each member of the team, professional-like, in the execution of his or her part of the ministry. As happy as I was to be a part, and eager to do a good job, I soon found myself struggling to get a firm grasp. I compared it to trying to jump aboard a fast-moving locomotive. I put my best foot forward, and had the best of intentions, but felt myself losing traction. I was so appreciative of the Pastor, for taking the risk to hire me, knowing I was still "wet behind the ears", and I wanted so badly to prove he had made the right decision in bringing me there. But it did not take long to realize that things just weren't going the way either of us had hoped they would. The learning curve was greater than I had imagined it to be, and I could tell my fruitfulness and productivity weren't up to the expected FBT standards. I truly loved the ministry there, and felt so honored to be a part of it, but there was just so much more to being a productive pastoral staff member, in a successful mega church, than I had realized. I kept reminding myself to hang in there, hoping it would soon get better. But I was not at all prepared for what was about to take place.

Fired!

One Thursday afternoon, probably six or seven months into our time at Florence, Pastor Monroe called me into his office. I went in expecting to be given a ministry assignment, or told of a family needing a pastoral visit. But, in no way, was I ready to receive the words I would hear.

"David, I'm sorry, but it just isn't working out", he wasted no time getting right to the point. "You're a good man, and I really like you, but you're just not ready for a ministry like this. If you know of another church you'd like to go to, I'll be happy to give my recommendation. Feel free to list me as a reference, but I'm afraid I can't use you here anymore. Go ahead and clean out your office before you leave today, and turn your keys in. Again, I'm truly sorry about this; I had hoped things would work out differently for you."

Meeting over….or so he thought.

I sat for what seemed like an eternity, in stunned silence. I gulped hard, finding it difficult to catch my breath – not completely surprised, but yet not wanting to believe what my ears just heard. Then like a flash, my mind zoomed back to Bud McCord's admonition, years ago, about knowing for sure, concerning God's will. And just as quickly, I thought back to the months of praying specifically, that God would graciously allow us move to Florence. The preacher had begun shuffling papers on his desk, waiting for me to exit the room, but I could not walk out of that office just yet. I simply could not leave it like this.

"May I say something?", I stammered, my mouth dry as cotton.

"Yes, of course", he seemed somewhat surprised.

"Preacher, I know I may not have lived up to your expectations so far, but I also know, beyond a shadow of a doubt, that God brought me here. And furthermore, I do not believe He brought me here for it to end like this."

My own words stunned me, as a heavy silence filled the room. I then sat back in my chair and waited for him to speak. He seemed a little taken aback with my response, but was undeterred in his decision.

"Well, you can think what you want, but go ahead and get your office cleaned out. Just let me know if you want a personal recommendation, and where you'd like me to send it." And with that, the meeting really was over.

Now what?

I went home that day, feeling like I was stuck in the middle of a horrible nightmare, from which I could not awaken, except this was no dream. I made a very strange and uncharacteristic decision not to mention a single word about the meeting to Debbie. For one thing, I simply could not bring myself to tell her about it, especially after all we'd been through.

The next day was my usual day off, and I told her I needed to go to the woods for awhile. Since my teenage years, I have often sought refuge in the woods, if I needed to be alone with the Lord for a serious time of prayer. I relish walking through the forest, enjoying the solitude of God's nature, and talking out loud to Him about the things on my heart. If there was ever an occasion requiring some intense "God and me time", this was it. I packed a lunch, placed it in my backpack, along with a bottle of water and my Bible, and headed out.

A good part of the day was spent talking to the Lord about what had occurred the day before. I reminded Him (as if He needed it) of the specific prayers He had answered, with regard to our moving to Florence; and asked Him for grace, wisdom, and strength, to respond to this situation, in a manner pleasing to Him. After a whole day of intense, heartfelt prayer, I drove back home with no real sense of direction. Nothing had really changed. I did not know what to do next.

Saturday was always a work day, spent making ministry visits to church members and prospective members, while making final preparations for Sunday services, etc. Because I didn't know what else to do, I simply went to work as usual. As I came into the office to pick up some visitation cards, and check my messages, I stopped by the coffee pot for a cup of "joe" on my way out. Ray, was the staff member with the longest tenure at FBT, and I had learned he was often Pastor Monroe's confidant on important church matters. As our paths intersected at the coffee pot, he gave me the strangest look, as if to say, "What are *you* doing here?" I figured he had probably been privy to my termination meeting. But neither of us mentioned it, and I went on, in a "business as usual" manner, without saying much to him. I stayed out of the office the rest of the day, never running into Pastor Bill...for which I was very thankful.

Sunday was like most other Sundays, except that I tried to keep my distance from Preacher. Saying it felt awkward to be at church would be a gross understatement. Early Monday morning I showered, dressed, and headed for work as usual, except for the fact that my stomach was in my throat. Monday mornings at FBT, were dedicated to a long staff meeting, led by Pastor Monroe, and usually lasting until lunch. Monday was also my hospital visitation day, which normally took up most of the afternoon. As a rule, we would all be in our places around the conference table when Pastor Monroe arrived for the meeting. Again that morning, I received a most unusual look from Ray when he saw me at the table. Then, when the pastor arrived, he also seemed very shocked to see me sitting in my usual place, but thankfully, kept his thoughts to himself, and proceeded with the meeting. I'll admit it was extremely uncomfortable for me, but I knew in my heart, it was where I belonged, even if no one else understood or agreed. Following the meeting, I quickly gathered my things, and headed off to the hospitals for my normal Monday ministry "rounds"(making sure they lasted the rest of the day).

With Monday behind me, without a confrontation, I went back to work the next day... and the next. I could not make anyone understand if I tried, but I knew I was where I belonged, and decided to keep on doing my job, trusting God to help me, until something broke loose. I can't say what was going on in Preacher's mind, but I suppose he just didn't know what to do with me. He had had the responsibility of dismissing a number of staff members over the years, but obviously never had one who refused to leave. Ironically, nothing else was ever mentioned to me about it, and gradually the strange looks began to diminish.

Days turned into weeks, and weeks into months, and I continued working and serving there, as if the firing discussion never took place. It was very, very uncomfortable, but I had to follow my heart, and remain true to what I knew God had placed there.

Harvest Time!

As I kept plugging away at doing what I knew God had led me to do, in a very short time, by His grace, my ministry at FBT began to take a very positive turn. There were no procedural or practical changes made in my weekly schedule; just a steady, unwavering continuance. I found it so difficult to concentrate on my work, and not be distracted by what had taken place, but just kept taking it a day at a time, while looking to God to direct my steps. It was doubly tough, because I had chosen not to even talk about it with my closest confidant…my dear wife. So I spent the majority of my work time "out amongst them", as I often called it, and minimized my time in the office, (which is how I prefer to do ministry anyway). Almost imperceptibly at first, but then with a steadily increasing visibility, I started becoming fruitful, productive, and effective in ministry. God began giving me eternal results for my labors, which became obvious to all…including Pastor Monroe. During the remainder of that year, I had the great privilege of seeing numbers of people, including whole families, come to faith in Christ, walk the aisle during the invitation, follow the Lord in baptism, join the church, and begin to serve at FBT.

Through relationships made in the community, I developed a growing pool of "prospects", whom God allowed me to reach for Him, and bring into the church, over the remaining years of my ministry there. Not only did God clearly validate that I was in the right place, doing what He had called me to do, but He began to use me powerfully, to help the church, and to advance His kingdom. And it did not go unnoticed.

A few years later, I received a very meaningful and rewarding surprise. I was publicly recognized, in an A.M. worship service, for being such a productive and effective staff member. As I was handed an unexpected thank-you gift, Pastor Monroe concluded his remarks to the congregation by saying, "…and this is the only staff member I've ever fired, who wouldn't quit coming to work."

My face turned beet-red, and the congregation laughed, though they didn't have a clue what he meant. Sitting there on the front row was my dear wife, Debbie, who didn't know what to make of the remark either. After church, when she could get me alone to herself, she pulled me aside and asked, "What in the world was that "firing comment" all about?" Only then did I finally share with her what had happened years earlier in the preacher's office.

God allowed Debbie and me to serve on the staff of FBT for nearly 14 years, before burdening my heart to move away and plant a new church, in a neighboring state. But I'll always be grateful for the way He allowed us to go to Florence, and the way He allowed us to stay until *He* decided He was finished with us there. I continue to have the greatest respect and admiration for Preacher, and remain so thankful for his willingness to give me some space, as God worked in both of our lives. The Lord taught me many valuable lessons through our Florence experience, which have stayed with me to this day: not the least of which is, that He is a God Who definitely answers prayer – sometimes in ways we never would have imagined. But then, that's not really all that odd...it's just our great, glorious, and very gracious God!

★★★

PUTTING A HANDLE ON IT...

1) *Three Important Relationships*

A dear pastor friend shared with me that every believer needs at least three spiritual relationships in his/her life. There should be someone who is like a Paul - a mature Spiritual leader or mentor; there should be a Timothy - a Spiritual apprentice, or someone being discipled; and there should be a Barnabus - a Spiritual encourager; someone who can always be counted on.

Who, in your life, lovingly but firmly, speaks God's truth into your heart? _____
_____

Who would you consider to be a mentor to you? _____

Who are you actively seeking to pour your life into, and influence for God's kingdom?
_____

Like Bud McCord's admonition to me, what are a couple of foundational principles you have learned, which help to guide you in your walk with God? (a) _____

_____

(b) _____

_____

2) *Our Father, which art in Heaven…*

On a scale of 1-10, how strongly do you believe God truly answers people's prayer today? _____ Can you recall any very specific prayers God has answered for you in the past year? (Yes / No)

If so, write out one or two of them here. _____

_____

_____

_____

What is a very specific thing, for which you are praying right now? _____

_____

What one word, in Jesus' discourse on prayer, (Matthew 21:21,22) indicates that we should pray *specifically*, rather in generalities? _____ One problem with praying in generalities, is that we have no way of actually knowing when/if our prayer has been answered. God delights in answering the prayers of His children, and when we bring specific requests before Him, we can rejoice in knowing we have received an answer from Him.

3) *Thy will be done on earth…*

Do you find it difficult to stand for what you believe, when others misunderstand, or even oppose you? List a scenario in which you have had to face this: _____

_____

Are you truly convinced it is completely possible to know if something is God's will or not? (Yes / No)

Write out what you would say to counsel a friend who asks you how to determine God's will for their life. _____

_____

_____

A verse in the Gospel of John, has often been a great help to Christians through the ages, when trying to determine God's will. Take a moment to read, and think deeply about John 7:17. Then list a few of the principles you find, in this verse, which could aid in discovering the will of God. _____

_____

_____

_____

At times His revealed will may seem somewhat unorthodox, but we must not forget just Who we're dealing with. Remember, God never violates His Word, nor His character, but neither does He necessarily conform to the way we think He should act or move. God doesn't fit in our neatly wrapped "box", nor would we really want Him to. Determine to do His will, to the best of your ability, as He reveals it to you, leaving the results up to Him. Spend time meditating on passages such as Proverbs 3:5 & 6 (one of the ones which has always sustained me), then seek to live each day in simple obedience to Him and His Word. It is amazing what God can do with people who choose to get out of His way, and let Him work the way He wants to. Who knows...the results may be out of this world!

Chapter Two

CALL AND CONFIRMATION

(Luke 10:2; Isaiah 30:21)

A Two-Fold Burden

Two things had been nagging at me for some time, and I could not get peace about either of them. I really needed some answers, as these two concerns seemed to wake up with me in the morning, and retire with me at night. They dogged me everywhere I went, and I desperately needed to reach some conclusions, in order to have some long, over-due relief. I needed to shed these two burdens, like a snake sheds its skin, but did not know how.

My wife, Debbie and I, had been serving on the pastoral staff of the Florence Baptist Temple for nearly twelve years, a role I found to be very fulfilling. We dearly loved our church, and had enjoyed a fruitful ministry there. We had just built our very first house, our three children enjoyed being enrolled in the church's Christian school, and life was good.

However, one of the two things that had been nagging me regarded the very church we loved and served. FBT was a tremendous and unique church in so many ways. A few years earlier, it had been featured in a best-selling book, written by a well-known Christian author, as one of the most complete, well-rounded church ministries in America. It was blessed to have a founding pastor, still very much engaged and effective, great Bible preaching and teaching, inspirational and top rated music (complete with full choir and orchestra), an exciting children's and youth ministry, a fully accredited Christian school, strong financial giving with very professional administrative practices, a growing congregation, and a veteran church staff - many of whom had been on board more than ten years. What was not to love?

But with all of these supremely positive features, one thing kept bugging me, about our church, and I had made several treks into Pastor Monroe's office to discuss my gnawing concern. The problem, as I saw it, was that our church had failed to reproduce. Simply put, we were not seeing people leave our congregation, to go out and begin other churches - neither in the States, nor in foreign countries. The Great Commission, i.e., the "marching orders" of every Biblical church, stated by Jesus Himself, could be paraphrased as follows. Healthy churches are to continually prepare and send people out of their congregation, to other geographical locations - both near and far. Those who are sent out, help others come to faith in Christ; then organize the new believers into Gospel-preaching churches. They then teach the new church to continue replicating this process. This is the type of reproduction Jesus desires every church to practice.

Bottom line - healthy churches birth other churches. I know on the surface this seems to go against the grain of some modern day church growth philosophies, because it emphasizes "sending out" rather than "gathering in". But at least two principles must be realized: a) although God chooses to work through local churches, those churches are to be Kingdom focused, and not just concerned about their own congregational empire; b) the law of sowing and reaping, in which God clearly tells us that anything we give to Him, with the right motive, will be given back, many fold. Add to these principles the fact that this has been the Biblical mandate ever since the New Testament era began.

So at our church in Florence, I was concerned that we weren't seeing this happen very often. Everyone was content to "stay home". Oh, we had seen a very small trickle, with two or three going out to start churches, spanning a twenty year period, but it was nothing close to what a church such as ours should be experiencing. And the more I thought about it, the more it ate at me, until I decided to make it the focal point in my prayer time. This then, was problem number one with me – our church was not reproducing.

The second thing that had been bothering me was not a church problem, per se, it was a *non-church problem*. In the case of the FBT problem, I was burdened that our church was missing a critical ministry element; while the second issue had to do with a *whole church which was missing*. Period. It just wasn't there; didn't exist. Let me explain….

In the Stanford family, Thanksgiving has always been a special holiday in which we all try to rendezvous at my parent's house in Pooler, GA. Mom and Dad look forward to, and prepare for the "invasion" weeks in advance. Everyone brings something to contribute, even though Dad always says, "Just bring your appetite." We set tables up, end-to-end in their spacious garage, and enjoy more good food than we ought to, while catching up on the latest family happenings. Once we're all more stuffed than the turkey, we converge in the den to watch football, catch a power nap, or just hang out together, enjoying each other's company. It is a wonderful time of family togetherness, which the Stanfords have cherished as long as I remember.

Following our family Thanksgiving dinner in 1997, Debbie and I decided we needed to go out for a walk. It may have been that extra helping of Mom's world famous macaroni and cheese, or a little too much of my sister-in-law's chocolate delight, but we felt the need to take a good, long walk. So we donned our sneakers and dutifully headed out. After all, I knew our services would be needed to help dispose of the leftovers in a few hours, so we thought it a good idea to burn a few calories prior to that event.

The town of Pooler had always been a lazy little spot in the road, just west of Savannah – mostly unnoticed for many years. Savannah is the city in which I was born and raised, but I hardly ever remember hearing much of anything about Pooler, though it is only 12–15 miles away from the heart of Savannah. It was one of those little speed-trap towns one would pass through, if traveling from Savannah to Statesboro, on Highway 80. But in the Fall of 1997, Pooler was starting to come to life, and it was evident that change was on the horizon. It was just beginning to be noticed, as a new Georgia frontier, and family-oriented subdivisions were starting to spring up all around, with many more in the planning stages. Savannah had become saturated with people, businesses, traffic, crime, etc., and to move east would put you in the Atlantic Ocean. So Chatham County was beginning to move westward, and the first stopping-off point was Pooler.

On that particular Thanksgiving afternoon, our walk took us through one of these newly developed areas located very near my parents' house. As we walked past block after block of freshly built single-family dwellings, I couldn't help but wonder which of the many area churches might be trying to reach these newcomers with the Gospel of Jesus Christ. Upon our return to the house, I posed the question to Dad, not expecting the answer I received.

"Dad, which church in this area, do you think will be attempting to reach the families moving into these new housing developments? In your opinion, which church seems to be the most outreach-oriented, in their ministry focus?"

"None of them", he replied, almost without batting an eye.

"What do you mean, 'none'? Surely *someone* has a heart for evangelism around here." I thought he wasn't taking me seriously.

"No one. None. Not happening" he continued. "Son, your mother and I have been living here for more than ten years, and no one has knocked on our door, invited us to church, or made an effort to reach us with the Gospel. What makes me think it will be any different for the people in those houses down the street, around the corner, or across town?"

I didn't like his answer, but couldn't argue with his rationale.

So with that discourse, nag number two began settling into my soul, and tugging at my mind and heart. I had been exposed to Christianity, and had become a follower of Christ at a young age, because of a church which believed and practiced the Great Commission. Throughout my growing-up years, our family had been highly involved in similar-thinking churches. The importance of reaching unchurched people with the Gospel of Jesus Christ, had been ingrained in me. Now I was brought face to face with the fact that my own flesh and blood lived in a town where this kind of church outreach seemed non-existent; and the growing number of unreached people in the area, had little hope of hearing the truth of God's Word from a committed church member in their area. I knew there were unreached people groups around the world, without a Gospel witness, but right here in the middle of the "Bible Belt"? It was too much for me to wrap my mind around.

Following our Thanksgiving visit, we headed back to Florence, and resumed our normal activities, but I could not get the two troubling issues off my mind. I would catch myself sitting on the platform of our church during worship services, looking out over the beautiful worship center filled with people, listening to inspiring, motivating sermons, being blessed by the uplifting music; and wondering why no one seemed to want to take these wonderful blessings we experienced each week, and deliver them to other places, so that people living there could experience them as well. Then my thoughts would switch from Florence to Pooler, with its fast growing population, which, by my Dad's estimation, had no church trying to reach them with the hope of the Gospel.

After carrying these dual burdens for awhile, I decided it was time to commit both issues to a period of serious, focused prayer. I began preparing myself to go into spiritual battle over these two issues, to see if God might step in and do something about them.

The Battle Begins

Throughout my Christian life, when facing issues requiring a higher level of prayer intensity, I had a long standing way to respond…go to the woods. I've always been an outdoorsman, and love going for long walks, spending time in the midst of God's glorious creation. Jesus often resorted to the desert, to a garden spot, to the wilderness, or up on a mountainside when He needed a special time of prayer with His Father. For me, it was the woods. I had a special place I would go, when I needed to be alone and have a serious talk with the Lord. With these two burdens weighing heavily on my heart, I determined it was "woods time". There, I could walk for an hour or three, talking out loud to the Lord about anything and everything. For the next several months, this would occur at least once a week − usually on Friday. During this time, as I walked and talked, my two primary and recurring topics of conversation with God were : "Lord, our church really needs to be sending people out to establish new churches", and "Lord, Pooler, Georgia needs a good church established, with a heart to reach out to its growing population."

It seemed that the more I prayed, the heavier the burdens grew, so after some time, it became evident that it was time to turn it up a notch. I was ready to move from serious to intense.

By now these burdens had become such a part of me, I carried them everywhere I went. I was becoming desperate to hear from the Lord on these matters. I had now grabbed hold of Him in prayer, and was determined not to let go until I heard from Him. I believed I was praying within the parameters of God's will, but I saw nothing happening to change either situation. The time had come to do more than simply pray about them; I needed to add *fasting* to my prayer sessions.

Fasting is a spiritual discipline which seems to have been mostly forgotten, or overlooked, by the majority of Christ-followers in my generation. Yet the same Bible which contains John 3:16, makes numerous references to the practice of fasting. Jesus told His disciples that certain prayers are only answered, when prayer is coupled with a time of fasting. Fasting means *voluntarily abstaining from food and/or other necessities of life, for a pre-determined period of time, for the expressed purpose of focusing one's spiritual energies on specific matters of fervent prayer.* During my Christian sojourn, I had fasted a number of times, for various reasons; so I decided it was time to do it again - on behalf of the *missing element* in our church at Florence, and the *missing church* in Pooler.

My Most Unusual Day

One Friday, after several sessions of fasting and praying, I found myself back in my cherished prayer-woods. I continued praying the same thing over and over, lifting my two burdens up to the Lord in prayer. I was busy pouring my heart out to Him as I had done numerous times before, when out of nowhere, I received a very strong impression on my heart or mind, or soul, or something. I'm not really sure where, in the body, impressions are received, but I received one – a strong one. It would have measured 11.5 on the impression Richter scale. Please understand that I don't believe the Lord speaks audibly to people today, (although He certainly could, if He wanted to, because He can do anything), but He does communicate in various ways. Being the infinite, all-wise God that He is, He has no problem getting through to us if He wants to relay a specific message... and He definitely knows how to come through loud and clear, if He so desires. This was one of those times for me. That day, as I walked and prayed, I was strongly impressed with these three words: "**What about *you*?**"

When the strong impression hit me, I became flushed, and my knees almost buckled.

"Do what?", I thought out loud. I must be delirious. Maybe it's the lack of food.

"What about *you*?" There it was again – clear and undeniable.

"Lord, are You speaking to my heart, or am I imagining things? I've been coming here specifically to hear from You, but I'm not sure what's happening right now. Are you just messing with me?"

"What about *you*?" It wasn't going away. Then it continued, "*you* could become the answer to both of your prayers, by going yourself to start a new church in Pooler."

I wanted to run hide, but there was no other place to go. I was already out in the thick woods. Sensing it really was Him speaking to me, about a task I felt very inadequate to do, I resorted to the *"but God"* syndrome:

"But God, I'm only an assistant pastor, not a lead pastor."

"But God, I'm not a very good administrator."

"But God, my kids are teenagers, and they wouldn't adapt well to the change."

"But God, have You noticed that we just built a new house?"

"But God, I'm quite comfortable right here in Florence, thank You very much."

"But, but, but..."

No response. He was having none of it. And the question, "What about *you*?" kept reverberating through my soul. Here I had been begging the Lord to do two ministry-related things - both for the good of others. I had been sincerely and fervently asking Him to do one thing in Florence, and another in Pooler. Then as only God can, He suggested a way to accomplish both objectives – utilizing one person...***me***.

I literally ran out of the woods, hurriedly fired up my little Bronco II, and pointed it toward home. I knew I had to go talk to Debbie about what I had experienced. Then I remembered I had promised to stop by a nearby artesian well, and fill up a couple of jugs, with delicious spring water to take home. On the way to the spring, following my Divine encounter in the woods, and culminating months of intensely seeking God, I became strangely aware of His presence with me. (I bet you didn't know God would ride in a 1990

Ford Bronco II, did you?) I was so thankful I had finally heard from Him, but there were still a lot of unanswered questions about the whole thing. I believed I knew what I was being instructed to do, but one thing was for sure…it would take an extra measure of His grace to make it happen. I certainly didn't feel like I was "pastor material", but I figured that part would have to be His problem.

He Wasn't Finished Yet.

Riding down Interstate 20, I reached over to turn on the radio. It was pre-tuned to my favorite Christian station, but my mind wasn't really on it. I was still shaken up by what had just happened in the woods. Suddenly I was aware of a song playing, which I'd never heard before. I turned up the volume, to have a closer listen. There was something about this song that profoundly connected with my soul. It had to do with the wonderful grace of God, and its total sufficiency for all of life's circumstances. The words were going straight to my heart, the sound track was beyond beautiful, and the singer seemed anointed. I found myself so enthralled with this song to the point that I began spontaneously praising God at the top of my lungs. Others passing me on the interstate, gave me some very strange looks and gestures; thinking I'd lost it… or smoked it… or something. I didn't give two hoots about what they thought; God was up to something. As the unusual song continued, wave after wave of intense love for the Lord began to sweep over me, and I began to weep uncontrollably. Pulling over to the shoulder of the road, because I could no longer see to drive, with cars and eighteen-wheelers whizzing past, I had a personal worship service, second to none. I did not want the song to end, but when it was evident that it soon would, I quickly scrambled for a pen and paper. If they should happen to announce the name of the song, I must write it down so I could obtain a copy of it for myself. There was no doubt, that I must have a way to hear this again, and play it for Debbie.

As the last strains diminished, I steadied myself and listened intently, not wanting to miss anything. I was praying, "Lord, let them say it; Lord let them say it." Then, just as I had hoped, the DJ then came on and announced the name of the song and the performing artist. Excitedly, I scribbled down every word, pocketed the scrap of paper, and headed down the road, feeling like I was transporting a very valuable treasure in my left shirt pocket.

Water jugs filled to their brims with fresh spring water, I finally headed for home. It had been quite a day – a Divine encounter in the woods, some intimidating instructions from God, and then a surprising song which turned me inside out. I was totally spent, wrung out, but enjoying the glow of knowing I had been in God's presence. But now, since hearing the special song, I had one more stop to make. Since my office was on the way home, I decided to stop there so I could call the radio station, while it was fresh in my mind, and find out how to get the album containing the song I had heard. For some reason I didn't have a phone with me, and I wanted to make the call to the station, before the radio personnel switched shifts. I needed to talk to the person who had been working when the song was played. Looking up the station's number I finally got a live person on the phone.

"Hello, this is David Stanford. I'm a regular listener to your broadcasts. How can I get information about a song I heard, a little while ago, on your station? I have the name of the song, but want to know what album it is featured on, so I can pick up a copy." (This was long before i-pods, e-tunes, downloadable music, etc.)

"That's easy", the friendly person replied. "If you have the date and approximate time, we can check our play-list, and give you exactly what you need."

"Super, I *really* need this song". I gave them the particulars, including the exact time it played, the title, and the artist. I was so thankful I had had the presence of mind to write it down, and since it had only been an hour or so earlier, I was confident they could help me.

After just a few minutes, the the DJ's voice came over the phone again. "Can you please give me that information again? I must have written it down wrong."

"No problem, I replied", as I shared the info once more.

When the radio worker returned to the phone the next time, she seemed confused.

"Sir, there must be some mistake. We did not play that song this afternoon. As a matter of fact, we've *never* played that song, because we don't HAVE that song on our playlist at all... nor any other songs by an artist with that name."

"Say What?!?! But I *know* I heard it less than an hour ago", I protested. "You *must* have it. Could you please look again?"

Another search revealed the same results. How could this be? How could I hear a song which had such powerful effect on me, and less than two hours later, the radio station tells me they've never even heard of it? This was so very odd. Then it hit me. No, this wasn't odd at all...it was so *very God*! I believe to this day, He miraculously sent that song through my truck radio, just to encourage me in the thing He had impressed on my heart earlier. It still remains one of the most poignant encounters of my life.

Sent Ones

God did confirm His call to me. I announced our decision to leave Florence, to go plant a church near Savannah, and our church family heartily agreed to back us with financial support and prayer. Today, by God's grace a wonderful, evangelistic church is thriving, on a prime piece of property, less than a mile from the very subdivision where Deb and I walked off our Thanksgiving dinner. And God used our act of obedience to start something in the Florence congregation we loved so much. I've counted no less than ten families who have also answered the call to go, and have been sent out of that congregation to start churches, since we stepped out, and made our decision public. Several went to begin ministries in other US cities. Still others left for places such as Costa Rica, the Philippines, the Orient, and Australia.

Yes, God is still on the throne, and His grace remains all sufficient. He tells us in Isaiah 55, "For my thoughts are not your thoughts, neither are your ways my ways, saith the Lord." (KJV) We often try to put God in a box, expecting Him to act in ways that make sense to our human reasoning. Rather, we need to understand that He is God; and as such, He can do as He pleases to accomplish His will. The best thing for us to do, is seek Him with our whole heart, then submit to Him with all of our being, leaving the results up to Him. He knows what's best, and has no trouble communicating it to us, if we will take time to listen. It is then that we discover His perfect will to be for our good, and His glory.

★★★

PUTTING A HANDLE ON IT...

1) *Our Divine Marching Orders*

Write out, in your own words, what is meant by the "Great Commission", as found in Matthew 28:19,20; Mark 16:15; Luke 24:47, 48; John 20:21; Acts 1:8 _____

_____

_____

_____

Is the Great Commission God's idea, or man's? _____Whose responsibility is it to carry out this mandate? _____ _____ List some personal ways you can be involved in helping to fulfill this command to those living in your world? _____

_____

_____

What is something you can do, this week, to be personally involved in World Missions?

_____

_____

_____

2) *Who, Me?*

God reserves the right to move us out of our comfort zone, in order to use us for His glory. (Agree, or Disagree?) What are some things, you feel you might be good at doing, in the service of the Lord? _____

What are some things you feel you could *never* do? _____

_____

_____

How did God respond to Moses, when he was told to do something, for which he did not feel suited? (Exodus 4:1-17) _____

_____

_____

In the end, what did Moses discover about himself? _____

_____

_____

About his God? _____

3) *Have Thine Own Way, Lord.*

Comprise a quick mental list of some of the people God chose to do His work, which are mentioned in Scripture. Interestingly, there is no stereotypical description of the kind of person God uses. What do you think God can do with a willing person who has the attitude, "it doesn't matter who gets the credit, as long as You get the glory"? _____

_____

4) *Say What?*

We know God speaks to His people through His Word. We also know that He will never speak to anyone, in any way, which is contrary to His Word. With that being said, is God limited in the ways He can speak to people today? _____. What are some ways God can and does convey His will to His servants, in our time? _____

_____

_____

List a few things, you might do, to keep your heart and mind open and sensitive to the Lord's promptings in your life? _____

_____

_____

Is there anything God seems to be impressing upon your heart, as you read this chapter?

_____

_____

Chapter Three

KASPER

(James 1:17)

The death of a long-time family pet, is never easy, regardless of the circumstances. And when I realized that our beloved Traveler had been killed, I immediately began gearing myself up, for what I knew would be a bad, bad scene at the Stanford household....as in *real* bad. Trav had come into our family some nine years earlier, through one of my hair-brained, super-fantastic ideas; and now, suddenly, he was no longer with us. I knew I needed to be strong for my wife, Debbie, and our three children. But he had been *my* buddy for nearly a decade, and who was going to be strong for me?

The Best Laid Plans....

Rewind the tape a few years. I had been out to visit Danny, one of our church members, who lived in the country town of Pamplico. There, I learned he raised and sold Smooth Haired Fox Terriers. Now, I've been a lifelong dog-lover, since the age of three, when my first dog, Fuzzy, shared ice cream cones with me from the ice cream truck. During my growing up years, I've enjoyed a wide range of pets, including several dogs and cats, gerbils and hamsters, turtles, a Palamino pony, a grey squirrel, a red fox, a black wild boar, an alligator, and many kinds of snakes.

But a few years after moving to South Carolina, my wife, Debbie, and I, had three young children, but no pets. I had been mulling over the idea of getting us a dog, and we were discussing which kind might be a good "fit" for our family. I had been very impressed with Danny's Fox Terriers, thinking they were extremely cool little dogs. They were active and playful without being "hyper"; small enough to go anywhere, but large enough not to get stepped on. They were extremely intelligent, even if they were strongwilled. To me, they were a good looking breed, with low maintenance coats. So, with all of the good qualities, I wondered why this breed was not more popular – at least not in our part of the country. I could not remember ever meeting anyone who owned a Fox Terrier, nor had I ever seen one, apart from Danny's dogs, even though I knew it was one of the oldest AKC recognized breeds.

So, as the wheels began to turn, in my short-circuited brain, an idea was formed, which turned into a plan. In one of my less-than-brilliant hatched-up schemes, I "suggested" to Debbie, that we could "kill two birds with one stone". Together, we could help promote this wonderful breed of dog, and put some money in our pockets at the same time, if we would simply enter the Fox Terrier breeding and selling business ourselves. Always the wise and prudent one in the family, she quickly pooh-poohed my wonderful idea, stating that we did not have the start-up money to begin a dog-breeding business. Nor was it our duty or responsibility to become the Fox Terrier poster family. She then hastened to remind me that I wasn't home enough to see to the needs, which would be generated by a pack of reproducing dogs, and she figured she knew who would wind up taking care of them. I knew in my heart, she was probably right on all counts. But not to be denied, I set about to carefully explain what a financially wise thing this would be for our family; and besides, it would be something the kids could help with as well, thus learning personal responsibility. I'm ashamed to admit I finally wore her down, but not before she prophesied that I would hear the words, "I told you so", at some point in the future. Ouch.

We did have to take out a personal loan from the local bank in order to start "the business", which consisted of materials to build a dog pen, dog houses, and supplies, plus, of course, the two dogs who would begin the whole enterprise, and put Smooth Fox Terriers on the map, once and for all.

Welcome home!

A trip to Danny's place brought about the purchase of Pete and Poppy, a beautiful pair of terriers. Poppy was almost solid white, with a black head and a few black spots sprinkled throughout her slender body. Pete was big and strong, for a "Smoothie"; mostly brown with a white face and a few white markings. Together they would produce a beautiful litter of tri-colored pups, which were sure to sell like hotcakes. I was getting excited already.

We brought Mr. and Mrs. P home and introduced them to their new surroundings. They really were great dogs, and I liked the idea of our three children, ages 5-11, being able to learn responsibility by helping to care for the dogs, and their future puppies. It wasn't long before Poppy was found to be in the "motherly way", and the countdown began. I was like a young father waiting for the arrival of a first baby. I made sure Poppy was well cared for, saw that her accommodations were as comfy as possible, and tried to wait patiently until the babies would arrive. Even Debbie's motherly instinct kicked in, and although she didn't want to admit it, she was starting to get excited about the new arrivals as well.

It's a boy….girl…boy….girl….

The birthing would begin late on a Wednesday evening. It was a church night, but I could tell the pups would soon be making their entrance into the world, and I couldn't get home fast enough to see how things were progressing. They began arriving, not long after we came home, and continued until the early hours of Thursday morning. I stayed nearby for each birth, making sure Poppy seemed to be doing okay. She was such a patient and attentive mother, right from the start, and I knew we had made a good choice when we selected her for our Momma dog. I was elated when the last one was delivered, bringing the final count to no less than seven little beautiful, wiggling, whining Fox Terriers.

I only got a couple hours of sleep that night, if that much, and was up "before the chickens", to go check on the new mom and her bustling litter. Unfortunately, one of the puppies had died during the time I was sleeping, but thankfully, there were still six. I went to work as usual, but later received a call from Debbie, saying that something was wrong with another one of the pups. By the time I arrived, two more had passed. I was getting concerned, so I contacted the vet, but he wasn't much help, and could find no cause for the three deaths. We made the decision to be thankful for the remaining four. But within 36 hours from the time Poppy started giving birth, we had to bury six of our precious new pups. I took some of their little bodies to the vet to see if he could tell me what had happened, but he still found nothing amiss. We prayed for the remaining pup to live, so there would be at least one left.

Out of business

I was so devastated and discouraged with the outcome of our venture, I decided, then and there, not to give it another go, and the Stanford Family dog-breeding business came to a screeching halt. The one living puppy seemed strong and healthy, so we chose to keep him as a family pet. Debbie was gracious, and refrained from saying "I told you so", even though I knew I deserved it, and Danny was kind enough to take Poppy and Pete back. Without the revenue from the puppy sales, it took us a long time to pay the bank back, which made me kick myself over and over, for not listening to my wife's wise intuition.

But on the positive side, we did end up with a wonderful pup of our own. The lone remaining puppy was actually the one I had considered the "pick of the litter" right from the start. He was a beautifully marked tri-color; predominantly white, with a black "saddle", a mostly black head, with a few brown patches sprinkled around, and triangle-shaped ears, which folded neatly to his head. He really was a perfect specimen of a Smooth Haired Fox Terrier, and it didn't take us long to fall in love with him. And, it appeared he felt the same way about being part of our family.

Traveler

Many years earlier, my maternal grandmother Hurst, whose maiden name was Lee, meticulously traced our family tree all the way back to the good General, Robert E. Since that day I had always taken delight in knowing I was a direct descendent of someone I considered such a great man of character and leadership in American history. From studying about him over the years, I learned General Lee's faithful horse was named Traveler; and since I didn't have a horse, I decided my dog would bear that name. The name was a good fit too, as our "Trav" turned out to be a bundle of energy, always on the go in search of new adventures; always willing to hop in the car for a ride to wherever it might be going, *if* the humans riding in the car could stand his breathtaking flatulence. (His were always "S.B.D.'s" with a strong emphasis on the "D".)

Traveler became a great family dog, and also my woods-walking companion. He was intelligent and eager to learn, though very hardheaded at times. I administered obedience training, and he did a great job of following commands…most of the time. His one besetting sin was his love of getting in a scrap with other dogs. Now don't get me wrong, he was not remotely mean or aggressive toward people. And neither did we ever, in the slightest way encourage his fighting; its just that when another dog came past the yard, he would break all the rules to try to get at it. While mowing the lawn or working in the yard, I could normally leave the gate wide open, even for a couple of hours, and he would obediently "stay". But if a stray dog happened by, no matter the size or breed, Ol' Trav was on him like "white on rice". And although he often came out on the "short end of the stick", he was not deterred. As good of a dog as he was, he had more bravery than sense. I do not remember how many times we rushed him to the vet to be stitched up… again, only to have him growling out the window, on the way home, if he saw another dog along the way. Other than his propensity for a brawl, he was an outstanding pet and faithful friend for many years – loyal and loving to the family he had become an integral part of.

Heartbreak

One Friday, which was usually my day off, I was hurrying to finish my yard work, so I could drop the girls off at the church for a youth activity. Not wanting Natalie and Emily to be late, I left my lawnmower and yard tools in the yard, came in quickly to shower, and then drive the girls up to the church. Deb came along for the ride. Upon returning home, I walked out on the back deck to view my freshly mown lawn, drink a glass of tea, and check on Trav. We were blessed with a large, open, back yard, surrounded by a cyclone fence establishing Traveler's boundaries. He was a dog who preferred living outside, rather than in the house, though the choice was his. So I made sure he had a comfortable dwelling, from which he ruled his domain. Usually, whenever I stepped outside on the deck, Trav was up there to greet me before I could get the door closed behind me. But this time something was different. No Traveler. I called, but received no response. This was most unusual. I stepped off the deck to look for him, and viewed something that made my heart sink. In my haste to get to the youth activity, after cutting grass, I had accidentally left the side gate open, and our beloved dog was gone. I called to Deb, and we began our search through the neighborhood, and surrounding areas. No luck.

We looked and called until time to go pick up the girls. I had no choice but to prepare them regarding what they were coming home to. We were all on the lookout as we drove back to the house. Just before turning into the entrance of our subdivision, I glimpsed a disheveled furry, white object, in the ditch to our right. Without thinking, I gasped, and Debbie picked up on it. I gave her the look that said, "Don't say anything". Arriving back at the house, I told Deb and the girls to go inside, and not come out. I then headed back to where I'd seen what I was looking for, but didn't want to see. There he was, apparently having lost a one-on-one encounter with a moving vehicle. I wrapped his body in an old blanket I had brought along, and headed back home to share the sad news of his demise, with the family. Everyone was in tears as I went to the back of our property to give my ol' buddy a proper burial.

A sad day turned into a sadder week, as we all missed him, each in our own ways. Deb later confessed that she would go out to his grave and have a good cry, while I was at work, and the kids were at school. On Thursday night we were about to fall asleep when I heard quiet sniffling coming from Debbie's side of the bed.

"Hon, what's wrong?"

The sniffling turned to sobs. "I – miss – Traveler, and – I – don't – want – Friday – to – come – because – it – will – be – one – week – that – he's – been - gone!"

I didn't say it, but I was thinking the same thing.

Joy comes in the morning…or, in this case, afternoon.

Friday did come, and once the kids were off to school, I told Deb that I was going to go to the woods for a little while. I was afraid it would be an emotional day for me as well, and I wanted some time to walk in the woods so I could think and pray privately. There was a special place I always liked to go, when I needed a time to be alone with the Lord, or to just think out loud. Usually Traveler was with me, but this time I would go alone. The place was also near a shooting range, which was seldom used during the week, so I often had the area to myself. I decided to take along a pistol, and some targets, so I could also practice my shooting while I was there, if I felt like it.

I spent some time walking through the familiar surroundings and sharing my heart with the Lord. Then thought I'd go over to the range and punch a few holes in some paper targets. Since I had not been hearing shots fired, I figured I'd probably have the place to myself. My figuring proved right; the range was deserted, just the way I liked it. I selected my favorite shooting stand and backed my Bronco II up to about twenty-five feet or so behind it, and began unloading my shooting gear – target stand, targets, tote bag, etc. My trusty Ruger .357 magnum was already strapped to my side. I placed my bag on the shooting stand - a wooden, bench-like affair, similar to the old-timey school desks - and headed back to the truck for the target stand, and my water bottle.

That's when I heard it, and froze in my tracks – a low, menacing growl, coming from somewhere nearby – sounding much too close for comfort. I had not noticed anything out of the ordinary, as I drove up to the shooting area, so this startled me. It was not uncommon to see wild animals in the area of the range, such as coyotes, fox, bobcats, etc., but I'd never been growled at before, and furthermore, I could not tell where the sound was coming from. I just knew it was close…too close.

Cautiously, I began walking toward the shooting stand and the growling began again, but sounded even louder. When I was twelve to fifteen feet away I spotted him - slowly walking out from under the wooden bench, coming toward me - ears laid back, tail tucked under, crouched low to the ground, lips curled, and teeth bared. It was evidently some kind of dog, and he had obviously decided there wasn't room for both of us there at the shooting range. I was inclined to agree. He continued steadily coming toward me, very slowly, still growling. I would be hard pressed to describe just how horrible this dog looked; like his life to this point, had been a continuous series of tragic events – anything but happy. My initial assessment was that he was an old, diseased mongrel, which someone had thrown out to die. Or, the thought occurred to me, he might be rabid. The second thought caused alarm. My concern was that I was many miles from the nearest human being, and should the latter assumption be true, and I found myself bitten, time would be of the essence. Prudence dictated that I slowly back up, ease into my vehicle, and give the range to the inhospitable, messed-up animal. But I did not want to leave my shooting bag there on the stand, and the snarling animal wasn't giving in, or going away. My senses were piqued, and I knew the situation needed to be diffused quickly. I unholstered my revolver, and retracted the hammer, just in case. With gun in hand, I then stopped my backwards walking, and stood my ground, to see what he would do next.

When I stopped backing up, and stood there with the gun pointed at him, he stopped too, no more than five or six feet in front of me.

"Old boy, I don't want shoot you, but I won't let you bite me out here in the middle of nowhere. If you come any closer I'll have no choice but to put you down." Then, as I took a closer look at the horribly disheveled fellow, I noticed that his teeth were pearly white, and his gums bright pink; indicating that this was not much more than a puppy.

"You're not an old man, are you, fella? And I bet you're not mean either – probably just scared." I spoke soothingly to him, hoping to convince me as much as him, as we continued eyeing each other. The growling had stopped, but he was standing his ground. Then I did something common sense would argue against. With the .357 in my right hand, still cocked and trained on the poor dog's head, I slowly went down on one knee and very carefully extended my left hand toward him. He began to cautiously approach my outstretched arm. Then, when he was close enough for me to touch, he did something I wasn't prepared for... he licked my hand. Relief poured over me. My suspicions were correct. This was a young dog which had experienced some very heavy trauma in his short life, and he had been taking shelter under one of the shooting benches. It was a gross understatement to say that he was in bad shape, and desperately needed someone to help him.

The mangled mutt seemed to sense that I was not a threat, and his whole demeanor changed, almost instantly. I began to speak soothingly and assuringly to him, as I petted him and looked him over. Never in my life have I seen an animal in such a mess. He must have been living and/or scrounging for food in the cornfield nearby, because he was absolutely covered in cockleburs. I don't mean he had a lot of them in his fur – he was covered – under his neck, in his ears, under his tail, in his "privates", between his toes, and all over his body. His thick fur looked like it had originally been somewhat of a whitish tone, but was now the color of red clay, and completely matted and tangled, from head to tail. It had probably been days since he had eaten, because under that orange, matted, cocklebur-infested fur was nothing but skin and bones. I wished I had brought something he could eat, but a quick search of the truck proved otherwise.

"Well fella, now that we're 'buds', I'm not going to leave you out here to die. What do you think about going with me?" I didn't have to ask twice. I gathered up my equipment, loaded it in the back and opened the passenger door. In he hopped, just like he belonged there. Seeing him in the seat next to me, I could not get over what horrible shape he was in, and he smelled as bad as he looked. I had no idea what I would do with him, but the animal-lover in me couldn't leave him out there for someone to abuse even more. I was glad I had refrained from pulling the trigger, though it had been an extremely close call.

On the way home, I began working out a plan. I would take him to our house and get some food in him, then off to our family vet, to have him cleaned up and inoculated. The next day I would take him to the Humane Shelter, where hopefully, someone would adopt him. As we rode together in my truck, his tail came alive, fanning his horrid smell toward me with every swipe. He stood tall and proud in the seat, and barked at passing cars, as if to say, "Look at me. Someone does care about me." The change in his temperament, from our first encounter was like day and night. Now he was acting like my best friend – only I wasn't sure I wanted to be seen with him.

I drove to our house and slipped him in the side gate, leading to the back yard, while I went inside to see if we had saved any of Traveler's food. Suddenly I was reminded that it had been one week, to the day, since I had buried my beloved pet.

"Honey, go take a look in the back yard", I called to Deb, as I rustled through the food pantry. She had been dreading the arrival of this day, because of the fresh heart-ache of Traveler's death.

She walked to the deck to take a look.

"WHAT IS IT?", came her startled cry. Not, "what kind is it", but *"WHAT* is it?" Honestly, this poor creature was such a wreck, she didn't recognize it as belonging in the canine family.

"It's a dog. I found him in the woods."

"If that's a dog, it is without a doubt the ugliest dog I've ever laid eyes on. What on earth do you plan to do with it?"

"Don't worry", I assured her. "I'm going to give him something to eat, then take him to the vet, and get him cleaned up and vaccinated. After that I guess I'll take him to the animal shelter, to see if some kind soul might adopt him. He's obviously had a rough life, and I couldn't leave him out in the woods to die."

The veterinarian's office said they could take him, if I brought him right away. They had no idea what they were in for. I was hoping no one would be in the waiting room, because honestly, I didn't care to be seen with this throwaway dog. Hope deferred. As I walked in with my new "friend", who was "just happy to be there", I received some very interesting looks, but had no trouble finding a seat, as the waiting customers moved aside and gave me plenty of room. No one wanted my disastrous dog near their manicured pets. The mangy mutt never stopped wagging his matted tail, and acted like he was running for Mayor. While many dogs hate going to the veterinarian's office, this one was just glad to be anywhere; anywhere, that is, but where he'd come from.

"We'll call you when he's ready," the receptionist told me as I handed him over and quickly headed for the door.

Total Makeover?

Just about the time the office was scheduled to close, I received a call from the vet saying that my pooch was ready. "He's not mine", I quickly reminded her, "I'm just helping the poor guy out".

As I paid the bill, the receptionist had to answer an incoming phone call. "Just a minute" she said to the person on the other end of the line. Then cupping her hand over the receiver, she said to me, "You can go to the back and get him yourself, if you want. He's in one of the holding crates in the back room."

A few minutes later I walked back to the receptionist's desk. "I don't see him, is there another back room he could be in?"

"No, he is there, go look again."

There were all kind of dogs back there, and they raised a chorus of barks, whines, and yelps as I approached. I looked through each cage, but did not spot the dog I had dropped off. One particular dog wasn't carrying on like the others, but was sitting, quietly wagging his tail as I came near. He was the only one with light colored fur. He was a beautiful dog – gorgeous thick white fur, now cropped fairly close, with a large tan splotch on his back, and matching tan ears. Could this be the same mongrel I found at the shooting range? It didn't seem likely, but no other dog back there even had the right color scheme.

I walked back to the front with the happy white dog tethered to me, by Traveler's leash. "Is this the one?" I asked.

"That's him. He's a real good-looker, isn't he?"

"Wow, I didn't even recognize him", I had to admit. I didn't leave the vet's office in the same manner I had walked in. This time I walked slowly to the car, not at all ashamed to be seen with the beautiful dog by my side. On the other end of the leash, the new furry recipient of the extreme makeover, had a new air about him, which seemed to say, loud and clear, "Life is good."

I knew our girls would be home from school by then (Nathan was away attending The University of South Carolina), so I headed home to introduce our overnight guest to the family. I had to admit, I was starting to like this guy, and began to hate the thought of taking him to the shelter. But at least he wasn't spending another night out in the cocklebur-infested corn field, and he would go to bed with a full belly … for the first time in who-knows-when.

I was amazed at how well mannered the white dog was. If I had to use a word to describe him, it would have been "grateful". It seemed as if he knew he had been saved from a life of horrible things, and given a new start, and he looked for any way he could show his gratitude. He was about the size of a Cocker Spaniel, with a tail that curled over his back like an Eskimo Spitz. His tongue was partially black, indicating he probably had some Chow in his lineage, and his markings were similar to that of a Fox Terrier. When cleaned up, he almost resembled a lamb, but he wasn't sissyish at all. He was just a cool, good looking, well mannered dog.

However, we learned quickly that he was deathly afraid of a broom or a fly swatter, no doubt a carry-over from his former life. In addition, he loved everyone he met, except young men approximately 18-21 years old. I also discovered shotgun pellets lodged under the skin in his neck. There was no telling what he had endured, and it gave me a sense of great satisfaction, to have had the chance to rescue him.

The girls took to him immediately, and Deb accused me of bringing home another dog besides the one she had seen earlier, saying, "There's no way that is the same dog." I told her about my interesting experience at the Veterinarian's office. Debbie and the girls collaborated, and decided he would be called Casper, but wanting to have some input in naming him, I changed the spelling to Kasper.

Fast-forward thirteen years, and as you might guess, Kasper still had not seen the inside of the Humane Shelter. He remained with us, and could not have been a better pet for our family. God had allowed me to find him, exactly one week following the unexpected death of our beloved Traveler. And though we didn't go looking for him, Kasper was just precisely the dog we needed, at that time, in our lives. He was protective, without being aggressive. He seemed to be filled with gratitude from the day I brought him home, and always did everything in his power to please us. We kept him indoors, and he never once had an accident on the floor. Never. And not only that, he was a good looking dog as well, with total strangers often stopping us to ask what breed he was. I could have answered, "Just choose one, and that's what he is." God, in His mercy and grace met the needs of a heartbroken family, and did it in a way we never would have imagined.

It was another very sad day when we finally had to make the choice to have Kasper "put to sleep", because of the many physical problems, he had developed in his old age. But we will always be thankful for the mangy mutt I stumbled upon at the shooting range. He brought nearly thirteen years of happiness to our family; and I have to believe, we were able to bring some into his life as well. As for Kasper's successor, Rose….now that's a whole different story for another time.

★★

PUTTING A HANDLE ON IT:

1) *Don't Judge a Book By Its Cover*

Have you ever been ashamed to be seen with someone or something that you thought might unacceptable to others, or make you look bad? What sin does that remind you of?

_____

God hates the sin of pride, yet it manifests itself in so many ways. Though Kasper was ugly and smelly, it was through no fault of his own. He needed someone to care for him, and show kindness to him. I misjudged him at first, but was glad I did not act on my initial impression. Aren't you thankful for God's love, which makes Him willing to take any of us just like we are; but is unwilling to allow us to remain as we are?

Who comes to your mind, that you may have misjudged, or been ashamed of in the past?

_____

_____

Are you willing to ask God to change your heart, so that your attitude will be different, in similar situations, in the future?

2) *"Man's Best Friend"*

We know God cares about people, but do you think He cares about animals s well? _____
Why or why not? _____

It is never right to mistreat or abuse an animal, for they too, are part of God's creation. Did you know God's Word even speaks about how we should treat our pets? Take a look at Proverbs 12:10, then paraphrase it, in your own words: _____

_____

_____

3) *Man of Sorrows, and Acquainted with Grief*

I once heard someone, speaking about the compassion of Jesus, make the statement, "No scene of suffering or sorrow ever escapes the Savior's eye." The Bible teaches us that God knows and cares when our heart seems to be breaking with sorrow. Psalm 147:3 says, "He heals the broken hearted, and binds up their wounds." (NASV) Whatever heartbreak you may be facing, or have faced in the past is of concern to the Lord. In the Book of Hebrews, Jesus is described as One "touched with the feelings of our infirmities" (4:15). How would you express this verse in your own words? _____

_____

Isn't it is good to know we serve a compassionate God, Who knows and cares when His people are hurting, or facing times of grief or sorrow? Even the sorrow which comes from losing a beloved pet. God truly knows and cares about all the details of our lives.

Chapter Four

IT'S NOT FAIR!

(Jeremiah 33:3)

"Aaarrrggghhh!"

"This just isn't fair", I muttered beneath my breath, as I angrily walked away from the dispersing crowd, and quickly drove away from the ceremony. In my vehicle, and alone with my thoughts, I began to contemplate what I had just witnessed, and tried to understand my unusual response to it. Was that really *me* saying those words? After all the times I'd explained to my children that "Life isn't fair", when they made a similar complaint. But this was different. This was about the Lord's work, and I was justifiably upset, because it really did not seem fair at all.

I had been attending a ground-breaking ceremony for the new YMCA facility, being built in the town where I pastored a newly formed congregation. And although I was happy for this fine organization to have a new building and grounds, our young, but growing church desperately needed a place to call home. A local businessman had donated fifty-two acres to the "Y" on which to relocate from their old rundown, outdated facility - the building in which our church was currently meeting each Sunday. I fully understood that a new YMCA building would be a good thing for our developing community. I also understood that because our church currently held services in the old location, we would also move with them into the new one when it was finished. That would be a welcomed change for our church. So I wasn't upset with the "Y"; I knew this was a good thing, both for them and for us, I just didn't understand why something like this couldn't or wouldn't happen for our church as well. After all, we were doing God's work, seeking to further His kingdom, seeing lives eternally changed through the Good News of the Gospel. *Fifty Two Acres*! That's a lot of land, and their primary function is to be a family-oriented organization, where people come to exercise, and children have a place to stay after school! Surely, if they can have fifty-two acres donated to them, our great God can find a way to give us some land. We don't even need fifty-two; I'd settle for ten, or even five. Fifty-two acres…what in the world did they need with that much land anyway? My mind wouldn't let it go.

My frustration stemmed from my jealousy to see God's work prosper and do as well as some of the local civic organizations and businesses were doing. As I drove from the ceremony I found myself "reminding God" that He created the entire globe, and all the land on it. It all belongs to Him – every acre of it. Surely He could move on someone's heart to donate some property to our church, as had been done for the YMCA. Yes, five or ten acres would be a great blessing, but why not fifty two? Why should God's work play second fiddle to other entities? After all, Who are we serving anyway? Whose work is it? Why not dream big dreams for Him? Is anything too hard for the Lord?

My wife, Debbie, was the unfortunate one who happened to be home when I arrived. She graciously allowed me to vent my frustration again, just as I had just done with the Lord. My attitude was not unlike the Psalmist, who in chapter 73 complained that the heathen prospered, while he and God's people suffered. (Not that the YMCA is a heathen organization, mind you.) In essence, the writer of the Psalm was also saying it wasn't fair. I fully understood where he was coming from.

A year or so earlier, Deb and I had left our position on the pastoral staff of the Florence Baptist Temple, Florence, SC, where I had served as associate pastor for 13 ½ years. We left, in order to answer God's call to birth new, baby congregation in Pooler, GA, a burgeoning bedroom community of Savannah. I was thankful to have the YMCA as a temporary meeting place for our church, even if it was a hassle to haul everything in each Sunday, in order to have worship services – chairs, sound equipment, nursery items, etc.; then pack it up and haul it all away again until the next time. Not only that, we were never able to schedule any kind of meetings during the week, because of conflicts with the Y's weekday and evening programs. I longed for our church to have our own place, where we could set our own schedule, and minister during the week, as God would lead us to do. A few weeks passed, and I received an unexpected phone call.

"Hello, David?

"Yes, this is David. How can I help you?" I did not recognize the voice of the caller.

"You may not remember me, but this is Don; Donald Wolfe. (I've changed his name in this story, for obvious reasons.) I met you in Florence, just before you moved away, and I've been following your new church's progress with great interest. Would it be okay if you and I have lunch together one day next week? I'll be passing through your area, and would like to meet with you."

I vaguely remembered meeting this fellow, several months earlier, but knew nothing about him. My intuition told me he was wanting to sell me something – life insurance, church furniture, a software program… something. But what could it hurt to meet with him, and see what he wanted? Besides, I figured he could catch me up on the latest news from Florence. So I agreed, and the meeting was scheduled.

Donald was a get-to-the-point kind of a guy, and I must admit I met him with my guard up. I surely did not want to get myself rooked into anything that was going to require more time or money – both of which were in short supply.

Once our tasty deli sandwiches were pretty well history, Don pulled a worn piece of paper from the middle of his legal pad. Before me, on the table, he spread out a very interesting picture, and invited me to take a careful look at it. It was a photograph, taken of a very long, hilly, winding road, which stretched out for miles and miles, over a rolling, country landscape. It was the kind of road I love to discover when I'm out for a leisurely motorcycle ride. The picture was taken at a certain point on the road, from which it stretched out before the viewer, like a long, narrowing, black ribbon, eventually disappearing over the distant horizon. But the desolate stretch of road was not the only object in the picture. Positioned in the photo, where the view of the road began, was a solitary man, dressed in a painter's white coveralls. He was kneeling in the middle of the road, with sweat dripping from his face. On the ground, beside his feet, sat a single paint can, with streaks of yellow paint running down the side. And in his hand the man held a paintbrush which had been dipped in the paint. In the foreground of the picture, where the road came into view, it was obvious he had been painting a double yellow line down the middle of the road. The line continued to the place where the painter was kneeling, and stopped there. Beyond him were miles and miles of plain, black asphalt, with no yellow stripe. As I quietly studied the picture, along with Don, its message came into focus. The poor man was attempting to singlehandedly paint a stripe down the seemingly endless expanse of roadway. It was an impossible task, and just sitting there looking at the photo, caused me to begin having feelings of anxiety and fatigue.

After Donald and I quietly studied the picture for a few moments, he broke the silence, "David, tell me what this picture says to you."

I thought for a few minutes before speaking. "Well, my first impression, is that this poor guy is in way over his head. Not only will it take him forever to accomplish this job, it doesn't seem possible."

"Very true, but look again", Don continued, "what do you think *it would take* for him to *be able* to complete the task?"

"Well, the first thing that comes to my mind is *help*. He needs a lot of help; he's trying to do it all by himself." I was now being drawn into the analogy. "Secondly, he needs *resources* – lots of resources. That one brush and can of paint won't do it."

As we discussed it further, we thought of several other things, such as an allotted amount of time, a workable plan to divide the work up into sections, regular breaks to help pace himself, a water jug to keep him refreshed, etc. But the one thing I kept coming back to was the idea of help. If the fellow just had some help; if someone else was in the picture; if he wasn't trying to go it alone, to me it would seem much more do-able.

Iron sharpens iron

Don sat back in his chair and took a deep breath, as he began to speak. "Dave, that's exactly why I'm here today. I have a proposition to make you."

"Uh oh, here it comes", I thought to myself.

"Dave, you obviously need help to establish a new church, don't you? I mean, you don't propose to do it all yourself, do you?"

"Of course not", I responded, "I *can't* do it all myself, nor would I want to. I've definitely got to have help."

"Dave, you need help, and *I* need help. Maybe we can help each other, and both be happy and successful."

"I'm listening."

Don continued. "You don't know me, but I'm a businessman. I have owned numerous businesses all over the United States. I have also helped several new churches get off the ground. Feel free to check me out, after I leave, to see if I'm telling you the truth."

"Okay, so how can someone like me help you? What do I have that you need?" He had piqued my curiosity.

"Well, the way I figure it, your church is going to need some property to build on, aren't you? I mean, you don't always plan to meet in borrowed facilities do you?"

"Of course we need property, but we're just a start-up church, with no funds accumulated yet, and only a few people. It will be years before we can hope to have a place of our own. But you still haven't answered my question about what I can do for you. I'm curious about that part of the equation."

"Dave, I just sold a large piece of property, in a state up north. And if I don't take the money from that sale, and put it back into another piece of real estate, I'm going to have to pay exorbitant taxes on it. You need a piece of land for your new congregation. If you locate a suitable piece of land, I'm willing to buy it, with the money I just received from the sale of my property. Then I will deed the land to your church, if you'll agree to write me an official letter stating that I donated the land to your church, along with its appraised value, for my tax purposes. That way, you'll have land to build on, and I'll keep from paying excessive taxes to Uncle Sam."

"Let me get this straight" I reasoned, with my brow obviously furrowed. I then repeated back to him, what he had just said to me, as he sat listening and nodding his head. I was waiting for the punch line, but it never came.

Now I know I'm not the brightest bulb in the chandelier, and all my life I've remembered hearing the phrase, "If it sounds too good to be true…." you know the rest. This had all the trappings of a "too good to be true" situation.

"I'll need some time to pray about it". I tried to sound spiritual. This was making me feel uneasy, and I was wishing I had brought someone else with me to meet with this fellow. There's safety in numbers. But Donald was unwavering. He seemed dead serious about this.

"Okay, Dave, go ahead and pray about it. Oh, and when you call Dr. Monroe to discuss it with him, you should know I've already talked it over with him myself."

"What do you mean? I never said anything about Pastor Monroe. I said I wanted to *pray* about it."

"I heard what you said, but I've also been checking *you* out, and believe I have you figured out well enough to know you'll call your former pastor before I reach the county line, on my way out of town."

Now I was feeling even more uncomfortable. How did he know I had already planned to run it by my Pastor, as my first course of action? This guy was slick.

We cleaned off our table, said our good-byes, and parted company. My mind was swirling with all that had taken place. I couldn't get the picture of the lonely, tired painter out of my mind. He made me think of myself, struggling to bring a new congregation to life and effectiveness. Then to have a stranger offer to buy property for our church, and give it to us with no strings attached…it was more than I could wrap my mind around. I couldn't wait to talk to my pastor about this. I appreciated the fact that, among other things, Pastor Monroe was a very astute business man himself. He would know how I should respond. Besides, I wanted to find out for myself if this Don fellow had actually talked to him, or if he was bluffing, to keep me from making that phone call.

"Dave, it sounds like a perfect win-win situation to me. I see no reason not to take him up on it", was Pastor Monroe's pointed reply.

"That's it? Just like that? You would just go along with it, if you were in my place?"

"Absolutely I would. It sounds like an answer to prayer, if I've ever heard one. Don't stand in the way of what God wants to do there, David. I think this is a great opportunity for your church"

Donald was pleased that I had talked to my pastor, and wanted to set up a second meeting with me. He was even more pleased, following the second meeting, to learn that our church had agreed to take him up on his offer.

The search begins

"Okay. Well, I guess the next thing to do, is to start looking for a piece of property. Let me know when you find one you like, and I'll come take a look at it with you. Oh, yeah, and before I leave, just to show you I'm really wanting to help you, here's a check I brought for you. I figure the church isn't able to do much for you yet, financially, so I thought I'd help out some. Remember our picture we looked at?"

And with that, he was off. I was left holding a sizeable check in my hand, and picking my jaw up off the ground. From that month, until the day our church was able to fully salary me, the checks from Don arrived regularly. He'll not know until eternity, what a tremendous blessing he really was to me and my family, at that critical time in our lives. This guy was for real, and it was looking as if God was about to do something special for our church.

This set off a bee hive of activity as our church members, excitedly panned out across our "Jerusalem" and began searching for a suitable piece of land. It was "all systems go" as we checked out every available parcel of real estate, which might serve as a good home for our young congregation. We wanted something that would be reasonably priced, centrally located, and would have room for us to grow and expand, as our ministry developed.

I was privileged to have my parents, as faithful members of our church. One day my Father, who was in his 70's at the time, was out taking a leisurely stroll down his street – a long street where the old, established part of town meets the newly forming subdivisions and businesses. He was a little more than halfway down the street, walking past a stretch of thickly wooded acreage, when he spotted it. Probably twenty five or thirty feet inside the dense woods, was a small, faded "For Sale" sign, no larger than a sheet of notebook paper. It had obviously been there for awhile, as the small trees and underbrush nearly hid it from view. Dad took down the number and brought it to me right away.

Land Ho!

A phone call later, and I found myself sitting in the office of a real estate broker, looking at a plat of the parcel of land. It was located a stone's throw from the brand new middle school and elementary school. It was within walking distance of several large subdivisions, which had been recently developed, with several more in the planning stages. It was only a couple of miles from the intersection of two major US interstates; I-16, running east and west, and I-95, spanning from Miami to New York. This would be an ideal location for any church.

True to his word, Don returned, eagerly approved the property, and made the purchase. Then he had the land sub-divided, so as to donate part of it initially, with the rest to come later, as the church grew some more. We were so excited, we couldn't contain ourselves. The property was perfect for us. But what excited me even more, was the fact that we would have plenty of room to grow and expand. We were already buzzing about the many different things we could envision doing with this land. The way I figured, it would take our fledgling congregation a few years to fill up that wonderful piece of property - - - all *__fifty-three acres__* of it! What an awesome God we serve!

★★★

PUTTING A HANDLE ON IT:

1) *It's Not Fair!*

In 2 Corinthians 10:12, Paul warns the Corinthian believers against comparing themselves with others. It is an easy trap to fall into. What are some ways we may find ourselves making these kinds of comparisons? _____

_____

_____

It is often easy for God's people to wonder why the lost world seems to prosper, and do well, while they continue to struggle. Be honest. Have you ever felt this way? (Yes / No)

Question – When we begin to feel this way, where is our focus? _____

_____

Where should it be? _____

2) *I Need Help!*

None of us can do the work of the Lord alone. But we all have something to contribute, and our gifts and talents vary from person to person. In my case, I needed someone like Mr. Wolfe to come by my side, and help in certain ways, which others could/would not.

What are some ways in which you feel you can contribute to the work of the Lord? _____

_____

_____

As part of the Body of Christ, we each have a function, or functions, to perform. When we each do our job, under the power of the Holy Spirit, the work gets done. Had Don not come along, and listened to the leading of the Lord in his life, I don't know how long it would have been before we could have obtained property, and built a church building.

3) *I have a dream!*

Too often we are hesitant to dream big dreams for the work of the Lord. Why shouldn't God's work be done in a big way? I surely understand that not all churches will become mega-ministries, but neither should we limit God with our small vision. Most churches make the mistake of thinking too small, rather than too big.

The prophet Jeremiah relays a message from God, to His people, about how He desires for us to approach Him. Look up, and write Jeremiah 33:3 here: _____

_____

_____

What kinds of things does God say He will show us, if we dare call out to Him?_____ and _____ things.

Read Matthew 17:20, and Luke 1:37. (KJV) Write down the one common phrase used in both verses.

_____

List some areas, in which you would like to be able to trust God for great answers to prayer. Think big; we serve a great God. _____

_____

_____

_____

Chapter Five

EMILY'S BLUE CAR

(Matthew 7:7-11))

"Dave, do you think we can turn it up a notch, and see if we can hurry and find a car for Emily? We really need ours to last a while longer, and at this rate, its days are numbered."

I knew my wife was right, and if I doubted her, all I had to do was take a stroll around our little Honda Civic. There was a huge gash in the back bumper, where Emma and a schoolmate had backed into each other in their high school parking lot, (with neither one of them at fault, of course). And now, the passenger-side mirror was dangling against the door, from a run-in with a construction cone which "they put too close to the road." Something had to give, but finding a good, dependable, inexpensive vehicle was not an easy task … especially on our budget.

Emily is the "caboose" of our three children - and by all accounts, our more "intense" child. She is an all-or-nothing; never-wonder-where-she-stands; living-life-large, kind of person. She had just started attending a college located approximately 4 ½ hours from our home, so we knew transportation was an issue we could not put off much longer. We had made the trip a few times, and Em had bummed several rides with another student who lived in a neighboring town, but she was eventually going to need a car of her own. I was dreading the idea of having to car-shop, but now but it was crunch time (pun intended).

Getting Specific….

"Emma, *IF* we were able to help you get one, have you thought about what kind of car you would be interested in?" I had to start the process somewhere.

"A blue one…dark blue…with brown or tan interior. Oh yeah, and I want a spoiler too. They're pretty cool."

"Well that really narrows the field. What about make and model, do you think that should be included in our search?"

"Something sporty…not an 'old person's car'".

"Okay, well that gives me a lot to go on. I'll start with the classifieds, and see what's listed there."

Looking for a car is the kind of activity that thrills some people – running down ads, kickin' tires, peering under the hood, dickering over the price, discussing features, etc. But for me, its like a form of torture. For one thing, I'm the kind of buyer they see coming a mile away. They *always* get me. I couldn't find a good deal if it bit me on the leg. My dad, on the other hand, is the world's best haggler. He can talk a person down so low they end up paying him to take the item off their hands, then they smile, and ask him to "come again soon" as he leaves with his prize. But in the case of his oldest son…me, the fruit *did* fall far from the tree…very far. So, several weeks later, the Emily-car-search wasn't making much headway, and I was getting discouraged with the whole process.

Hello???

One particular Monday, following busy day of ministry, I dashed into my office for a minute before heading home. I was pastoring a newly established church, in a small town near Savannah, GA. On this particular day, it was nearly the time that Deb would have dinner prepared, and I still had more visits to make, later that night. I thought I'd take a minute to swing by the office and check my phone messages, before heading home to wolf down my supper, then turn around and go right back out again. We were preparing to build our first permanent church building, and I was giving it my all, to keep the newly formed congregation growing and moving forward. It seemed like there were never enough hours in a day.

"Beeeeeep", the answering machine indicated it had recorded some calls during my absence. I pressed the appropriate button, to listen to the messages.

"Hello, this is Cindy. Sorry I missed you. I'm returning your call from this morning. Feel free to call back when you get in."

"Cindy? Cindy who? I didn't call a Cindy today. She must have called my number by mistake."

I started to just delete it, but thought I should at least let her know she left the message on the wrong person's phone. I took down her number, dialed, then waited, rather impatiently, as it began to ring.

"Hello?"

"Hi, Cindy?"

"Yes? Who's calling?"

"Cindy, this is David Stanford. You left a message on my phone earlier today, saying you were returning my call, but I didn't called you. I think it must be a mistake. Just thought you'd like to know, in case you were trying to reach someone else."

"No, there's no mistake", she quickly replied, "I have your number right here on my phone. Is it 748-2022?"

This was odd. "Yes, that's my number alright, but I promise I haven't called you. Not today, not ever; I don't even know you. I'm not sure how that could have happened, but evidently it did…if you say so. Some fluke, I guess. Sorry to bother you."

"Well, okay, then, no problem. I just figured you must have been someone calling about the car. Have a good day."

"Car? Did she say Car? W-W-Wait a minute, Cindy. Don't hang up. Cindy, are you still there!?!?"

"Umm yes, why?"

"Did you say something about a car?"

"Yes, I said I thought you were someone calling about the car I have for sale."

"You have a car for sale? I had no idea."

I was beginning to get a strange feeling about this phone call. What was going on here? Was someone going to step out from behind the door and yell, "Smile, you're on Candid Camera!"? But since I was into it now, I might as well push a little farther.

"Cindy, can I ask you a question about your car?"

"Sure, what do you want to know?"

"Just out of curiosity, what color is your car?"

"What color? Most callers want to know what kind it is, and how many miles are on it. But oh well, its blue… sort of a navy blue."

"And would it happen to have tan interior?"

"How'd you guess? Yes, it has tan leather seats. And for the record, it's a Saturn, SR2."

"Those are kinda sporty, aren't they?"

"Yes they are. Actually it's a two-door sport coupe, with a sun roof and a spoiler."

"Cindy, could I arrange to see your car?"

"I thought you weren't looking for a car."

"I never said I wasn't looking for a car; I said I didn't *call* about your car…and I didn't. Still don't know how that happened, but since we're talking about it now, I'd like to take a look at it. Actually I *am* looking for a car, something like the way yours sounds, for my daughter."

Love, at first sight

We arranged a meeting, so we could look at, and test drive the blue car. As it turned out, it was the perfect ride for Emily, and served her well during the remainder of her time at college. Cindy happened to be a local school teacher, and was thrilled to be selling the car to someone seeking to further their education. It was a win-win situation, all the way around. Cindy made her sale, Emily got her car, Debbie got hers back, and I put forth my best Dad imitation, which persuaded her to knock $500 off the price. To this day, none of us have a clue how my phone number found its way to Cindy's message box, but nevertheless, our car searching days came to an end that day, and everyone was happy with the outcome.

★★★

PUTTING A HANDLE ON IT:

1) *God Knows Your Needs*

What need do you have in your life right now, that God is ***not*** fully aware of? _____

_____

Do you think He knows the desires and longings of your heart as well? (Yes / No)

Why do you think many Christians are hesitant to spell out their heart's desires, in prayer?

_____

_____

2) *God Knows Your Limitations*

God was aware that we needed our daughter to have a car. He was also aware of how difficult it is for me to deal with salespeople, not to mention our financial situation.

Like my problem dealing with salespeople, is there a normal, everyday function of your life, you find distasteful or difficult? _____

Does the One Who knows you better than you know yourself, know about this too? (Yes / No)

3) *God Knows Your Number*

I am fully aware that the circumstances of this story are the exception, rather than the rule. But I am also fully aware that God knows how to get ahold of any of us, any time, and in any way He chooses. He knows our number, and is not afraid to dial it.

List some instances in the Bible, where God supernaturally worked in someone's life, to give them a message, or to get their attention.

- _(example): He spoke to Moses through a burning bush in the desert_ ___
- _____
- _____
- _____

4) *God Knows How to Orchestrate Your Circumstances*

Our God is the God of inexhaustible wisdom and creativity. There are many instances, recorded in Scripture, in which Divinely arranged circumstances resulted in the intersection of two people's lives, who never planned to meet each other. We often refer to these instances as Divine Appointments. Can you think of a Bible example, in which a Divine appointment took place? (There are **many** to choose from.) List the event you select here, as well as the Scripture passage in which it is found. _____

_____

_____

Can you think of a time in your life, in which a Divine Appointment took place? _____

_____

_____

Looking back at this circumstance, how did it work out for your good, and God's glory?

_____

_____

_____

During your quiet time this week, ask the Lord to open your eyes, so that you will be fully aware of ways He is working in your life right now.

Chapter Six

THE LATE GREAT SERMON SWITCHEROO

(Isaiah 55:8, 9)

Ahhhhh, how sweet it is.

Those who know me best, sometimes call me a procrastinator. I prefer the term "organizationally challenged", and it often manifested itself when it came to protecting my weekly study time. As the pastor of a new, growing, church, I struggled to finish my sermon preparations early in the week, and too often found myself staying up late on Saturday to wrap things up. (Hey, confession is good for the soul, right?) But it had been a good week, and on this particular "Sunday eve", I was feeling pretty confident about the next day's sermon. Rather than late-night cramming, I could simply relax, calmly pour over my notes one last time, and spend some extra time in prayer, before hitting the sack.

Satisfied it was all in order, I placed my neatly-typed Sunday message notes in the three-ring binder I used each Sunday, put the binder in my briefcase, sat the briefcase by the door, and headed off to the bathroom to brush my teeth. It felt good to have done it right this week. With toothbrush in hand, I thought, "This is the way it should be each week. Make a mental note to spend some time working on the weekly schedule, so as to insure this happens more often." Dental hygiene complete, it was time to rest my mind and body for a busy Lord's Day, which would begin in a few hours.

Not so fast, son

Then, out of nowhere, it happened. Just as I was slipping between the awaiting covers, I was aware of a very strong impression flooding my mind and soul. There was no audible voice, no flashing lights or blowing wind…just a very strong, sudden and clear impression which could not be ignored. It seemed to say something to the effect of, *"That's not what I want."*

Do what? Where did *that* come from? Have I started dreaming already? Surely I must be imagining things. I guessed my tired mind must be playing tricks on me. After all, I was pretty exhausted. So I decided to dismiss it from my thinking, and go on to sleep… or so I thought. But the strange message continued to pummel my mind. *"That's not what I want. That's not what I want."* Not only was it not going away, it was growing in intensity. This wasn't good.

By now I was wide awake again, and knew I wouldn't be able to simply ignore whatever this was, but must deal with it, one way or another, if I hoped to get some sleep. Throughout my Christian life and ministry, I have always tried to cultivate a sensitivity to the promptings from the Lord; to keep my spiritual antennae tuned to His Divine guidance and direction. But I also know there are those who get worked up in a lather, with the whole "hearing-from-God thing". Some say God speaks to them through voices, through visions, etc. To me, most of that is as phony as a three dollar bill. God has given us His completed revelation, called the Bible, and it is the primary way He communicates to His people today. However, I also know that God is not limited or bound to any one thing, and being the Sovereign God of the universe, He can do as He pleases to get our attention… or to send us a message. And sometimes, He chooses to communicate in ways we may not be expecting.

On this particular night, I knew my "impression" could be coming from one of two sources – either God was communicating a message to me, or the enemy, Satan, was trying to derail me from getting the rest I needed, and/or preaching what God had laid on my heart. I decided to take it to the Lord in prayer, and seek to clear this up, once and for all.

I didn't bother Debbie, but slipped quietly out of bed and went out to the kitchen/dining area where I could think and pray.

Please make it known

"Lord, if this impression is from You, I need to know for sure. You know I've worked hard to prepare the message I believe you want me to preach tomorrow, and I feel like I'm ready to do so. So, if You're telling me that's not what You want, then please tell me what

You *do* want. I'm willing to listen, and do what You want me to do, but I need to know what it is. I need You to clarify what I am to do, and I now await Your answer."

I sat, waiting in the dark silence for half an hour or so, trying my hardest to remain keenly sensitive to His leading.

Nothing.

Feeling like I'd done all I could do, I said to myself, "Okay, well I guess I must have been mistaken. Looks like they'll get the one I've already put together. Time to finally get some shut-eye."

But before my tired body had time to warm the cool sheets, my mind was smitten with yet another strong impression. *"Five Fearful, Frightening Facts."* This time, it was a no-doubter.

You could have knocked me over with a feather. "Five Fearful, Frightening Facts? Where in the world did *that* come from? Are you kidding me? This is too weird." I was beginning to feel spooked now.

Approximately fifteen years earlier, when I was first employed as a pastoral staff member of the Florence Baptist Temple, in Florence, SC, Pastor Bill Monroe had preached a message entitled "Five Fearful, Frightening Facts". As I usually do, when listening to someone preach, I had scribbled down the outline on a scrap of paper and stuck it in my Bible. I was very impressed with the sermon, so a few days later, I asked Jane, the Pastor's secretary, if she could get me an actual copy of the sermon notes for my "file", which she did. (Jane could find anything. The proverbial needle-in-the-haystack wouldn't stand a chance with her.) When she gave it to me, it was a simple, hand-written outline, on a half-sheet of typing paper. I thanked her, and stuck it in a folder, along with many, many others, which I had gathered over the years. Once it went in "the drawer" it was out of sight and out of mind.

But on this particular Saturday night, my mind went back to that sermon I had heard so many years before. I've literally heard thousands of sermons over the past twenty or so years, and the vast majority of them are long since lost, in my fading memory banks. But that particular sermon was one that had stuck with me, even though it had not actually crossed my mind, in I-don't-know-how-long. It did have a catchy title, and I've always been a sucker for alliteration, so I vaguely remembered the gist of it. But now as I tried to summon all my powers of memory, I could not, for the life of me, remember any specific part of the outline, Scripture passages, major points, or anything else about it. I had hit a brick wall…in the middle of the night, with Sunday morning only a few hours away, and the clock ticking.

The perils of procrastination

Some people are "filers" and others are "pilers". My dear wife says I'm the poster child for the latter category. In my office file-cabinet I had two special drawers labeled "To be filed". They contained sermon notes, illustrations, poems, articles, etc., which I have collected from various sources, over the past 25 or 30 years, thinking I may use them….one day. These drawers had no degree of organization or order, and they were both jam-packed, front to back, as tightly as they could be. For years, I kept saying I needed to organize and file these properly. (Did I mention I've been called a procrastinator?) *If* I still had a written copy of that particular sermon, and that was a big "if", it would most likely be stashed somewhere in one of those drawers. This was truly a "needle in the haystack" situation, and calling Jane was out of the question at this time of the night. Realistically, it could take hours to try to find anything in those drawers, and now it was nearly midnight. I could get dressed and go up to the church, to search for it, but that would mean getting back to bed in the wee hours of the morning. And our morning worship service began at 9:30.

After pondering the situation for a few minutes, I made a conscious decision to put it back on the Lord, just like He tells us to do in Psalm 55:22, 1 Peter 5:7, and other places.

Cast your care on Him

"Lord, I feel like You've spoken to my heart tonight about this matter. I sense You are leading me to change the sermon for in the morning, but I have no idea where my copy of that sermon is, or if I even still have it. And besides, it is quite late (although time means nothing to Him). If I am understanding You properly, and You are truly impressing upon my heart, to preach 'Five, Fearful, Frightening Facts' tomorrow, then You're going to have to let me either find, or remember the outline. I am willing to obey, but right now, there's not much I can do about it. Therefore, I'm planning to go to sleep, and we'll see about it in the morning."

With that I went straight to bed, and slept like a stone statue, until the alarm clock notified me that a new day was about to begin. Little did I know what a day it would be.

Time for You to work, Lord.

My first conscious thought, after shaking out the cobwebs, was about the mysterious sermon outline. But I tried not to panic or stress over it. I had given it to the Lord, and now it was up to Him to act on my behalf. I showered, dressed, and made a stop at Cracker Barrel for a fresh, hot, cup of joe, on the way to the office. Strange as it may seem, I had an unusual peace about this situation, believing that the Lord had impressed these thoughts on my heart, and trusting that He would work it out, in some way. Arriving at the office, I put my things down and went straight to the closet containing the file cabinet, which I hoped, still held the needed sermon notes. Before touching the cabinet, I knelt down on the floor before it, and once again, committed the situation to the Lord.

"Lord, our service begins in a couple of hours, and it could easily take that long to go through these drawers. If I've heard you correctly, then guide me to the piece of paper I need to find."

"Eeney, meeny, miney, moe; pick a drawer and have a go". I literally selected one of the two crammed drawers, and opened it all the way. Then, without looking, I parted the contents, right down the middle, and reached in to grab a fistful of papers, to begin sorting through. As I extracted the random scraps from the drawer and turned to go sit at my desk, my eyes glimpsed the paper lying on top of the stack. Written across the top of the ½ sheet of typing paper, in Bill Monroe's handwriting, were the words, *"Five Fearful, Frightening Facts."* Immediately, the hair on the back of my neck stood at attention. Could this really be happening?

Now I'm not the sharpest knife in the drawer, but it was obvious that God was up to something. All I could do was kneel before Him, on the spot, and genuinely thank Him for His goodness. I then put the rest of the papers back in their hiding place, and walked to my desk, clutching the scrap of paper like it was a valuable treasure…which to me, it was.

I read over the simple outlined message, taken from the sobering passage found in the seventh chapter of the Gospel of Matthew. In this passage, spoken by Jesus, the readers are warned, "Not every one that saith unto Me, 'Lord, Lord,' shall enter into the kingdom of Heaven." (KJV) It goes on to say that there will be many, who, relying on their religious practices, good works, etc., will be eternally disappointed. Sadly, they will find out too late, that they were trusting the wrong things to get them into Heaven. To me, it is one of the saddest, most poignant and powerful passages in the Bible.

I took the piece of paper just as it was, stuck it in my Bible, and moved over to my "prayer chair", a nice Lazyboy recliner, one of our sweet church families gave me as a moving-in gift, when we occupied our new church building. It was where I loved to kneel and pray, when in my office. I knew God was definitely at work that morning, so I simply tried to commit myself entirely to Him and His purposes. The time for the service to begin could not arrive soon enough for me, on that day.

When God calls the shots, good things happen.

When the time came for me to preach, I simply went through the outline written on the paper before me, without embellishment. I knew that whatever occurred that day, would be God's doing, not mine. I was simply trying to follow His lead. The sermon ended sooner than mine usually do, and I began the invitation, encouraging people to follow God's promptings in their lives.

Almost immediately, a middle-aged man who was visiting our church, stepped into the aisle, and made his way to the front row of seats. Right behind him, came his wife, wiping away the tears. I met them in the aisle, and asked them why they were coming. Both said they knew they needed to receive God's gift of eternal life, so they could be sure of going Heaven one day. I thanked them for coming, and handed them off to an altar worker, so he could share Scripture and pray with them. At that moment I saw a young mother heading toward the front of the building, also with a tear-stained face. She too, said she wanted to trust Christ as her Savior. So I had someone pray with her as well. The presence of God was heavy on that service, as many others came forward for various reasons; with numbers of them weeping openly, as God dealt with their hearts.

The three visiting adults who trusted Christ that day, went on to be baptized, and become faithful, contributing members of our church. I still love all three of them dearly, to this day. I've never had anything quite like that happen in 34 years of full-time ministry. God decided to pull a sermon switcharoo on me, proving once again that He is the One in charge. I am so thankful I had the presence of mind to listen to Him, and follow His leading that day. I wish I could say I have always been that sensitive and obedient to Him.

Years ago, I remember hearing someone say, "Man proposes, but God disposes." We may think we have it all together, but He is the One Who makes it happen, as we yield our all to Him, and remain sensitive to His will.

★★

PUTTING A HANDLE ON IT:

1) *The place of preparation*

Do you think God's work requires planning and preparation? (Yes / No) An old saying goes, "if anything is worth doing, its worth doing well." How much more should this apply to the work of the Lord! What are some ways we might justify our failure to adequately plan and prepare to do God's work? _____

The truth of the matter is, God deserves our best, and our best is usually not achieved when we "fly by the seat of our pants", or throw things together at the last minute. (Agree, or Disagree ?)

Take a moment to read the following verses, then write out each one, in your own words: (Colossians 3:23) _____

_____

(1ˢᵗ Corinthians 10:31) _____

_____

2) *Where He leads me, I will follow…*

One of the great disciplines of the Christian life is learning to live with sensitivity to God's leading. Though planning and preparation are very important aspects to serving God, He is still God – the sovereign God of this universe. And if He chooses to change directions, without giving us prior notice, it is His prerogative. Cultivating a sensitive spirit to God is a sign of spiritual growth and maturity. We should understand and agree, that God can interrupt our lives anytime He pleases, when He wants us to go a different way or choose a different path. Like our supreme example, Jesus Christ, we should often be heard to say (and mean it), "not my _____, but _____ be done." (Luke 22:42)

3) *Two Eternal Things*

Do you realize that there are only two things on this earth, which we can touch with our lives, which are eternal? ***Only two***; not six, not eighty-seven, not a thousand. The only two things we have on earth, which will be with us, in Heaven, for all eternity, are the Word of God, and the Human Soul. God's Word (eternal thing #1) is what He uses to affect the Human Soul (eternal thing #2). So when He chooses to bring the two together, in ways we might not have planned, its okay. And anytime we have the privilege of being involved in this process, we can know, we have accomplished something of eternal value.

List some practical ways you can be involved with these two eternal things, in your life now:

- The Word of God – _____
  _____
  _____

- The Human Soul – _____
  _____
  _____

4) *The Lord of the Harvest*

One of the things God calls Himself, in Scripture, is the Lord of the Harvest. This description of God reminds us that he is like a farmer, looking over his fields, making sure everything is done, which will perpetuate a bountiful harvest. God knew exactly who would be present in our church service on the day of the "Late Great Sermon Switcheroo", and He also knew what they needed to hear, which would best speak to their hearts. I thought I had the right sermon prepared for the day, but the Lord of the Harvest, in His wisdom, knew a different tool was needed on that particular day. And when we step aside and let Him call the shots, good things happen. He is much more concerned about the souls of men than we will ever be, and sometimes He may choose a different implement than what we expected, to bring about the harvest. If we are more concerned about His Kingdom than about our little plans, then we'll be glad for the interruption, and thankful for the results.

Chapter Seven

THE RING

(Psalm 50:15)

A Dream Come True

We finally did it. After years of wanting to, hoping to, and dreaming about it, my wife, Debbie, and I, took our first motorcycle trip to the mountains. Ol' Goldie, our canary yellow 1996 Kawasaki Vulcan, had become our therapy, during years of non-stop ministry involvement. We could fire her up, and head off for an hour or three, with no cell phone, no problems to solve, no needs to be met, no questions to answer. Don't get me wrong; it wasn't that we didn't enjoy full time ministry, but everyone needs an occasional break. Why, even Jesus told His disciples to "come apart and rest awhile", at one point in His earthly ministry. So when Deb and I could not really go away, Goldie was always ready and willing to provide a short get-away.

But on this particular occasion, we had been talking about how we wanted to celebrate our upcoming 33rd wedding anniversary. And since we were married in the month of July, (actually 7/7/77, at 7:00, with seven bridesmaids and seven ushers), we figured that would be a good month for our first two-wheeled, out of town road trip. Hendersonville, NC, became our destination of choice, and we eagerly began planning the details of the trip, which could not arrive soon enough.

The trip to the mountains took longer than expected, so we arrived in time to unload the bike, grab a bite of supper, and call it a day. The next day was to be spent exploring some of the many fabulous mountain roads dissecting and intersecting western North Carolina, a true motorcycle paradise. The primary focal point for the day was to be Mt. Mitchell, the highest peak in southeastern USA. The day turned out to be all we had hoped it would be; with superb weather, breathtaking scenery, quaint mountain towns, and a delicious lunch in the small restaurant nestled atop the mountain. After one more jaunt down a section of the Blue Ridge Parkway, we headed back to Hendersonville, and our awaiting motel, where we could unwind and enjoy recounting an anniversary which was sure to be fondly remembered. But little did we know just how memorable it would become before it ended.

We had planned to not venture back out that night, so as to rest up from a long day in the saddle. But knowing out time was limited, and that we had to head back home the next day, we opted for one more dusk ride, to grab a cup of coffee and a snack. The clerk at the Mountain Inn was more than helpful, as usual, with directions to a recommended coffee shop. Goldie roared to life again, and we were off, smiles plastered across our faces. Soon, however, the prescribed route deteriorated into a road construction site, which then led to a "road closed" sign. Time for "plan B". I thought I knew another way to get where we wanted to go, so a U-turn, a little backtracking, and we were off again. But within minutes, the blue sky began taking on an increasingly grayish hue. A few more miles, and I felt the first drop. Mission aborted, we high-tailed it back to the motel, not wanting to endure a rain soaked ride, if we didn't have to (been there, done that, got the T-shirt).

Disaster!

Back at the room, we soon realized just how tired we really were, and thought it best to call it a day. But even without the evening ride, it had been a great day on the bike, and a superb first trip to the mountains. I decided to try to catch some of the Atlanta Braves game on TV, while Deb stepped into the restroom to begin the "makeup removal process", a nightly pre-sleep ritual which would give me time to enjoy a few innings of the game. I settled in, remote control in hand, ready to enjoy some baseball. But before I had time to get the soft chair warm, the blissful quiet was shattered, with a mournful shriek, "***My ring*!!!**"

"What about your ring?", I was almost afraid to ask.

"My wedding ring…it's not here; I don't know where it is", came the anguished response.

In my most re-assuring tone, I replied, "Now Honey, it has to be here somewhere. When do you recall seeing it last?"

The only thing she could remember was that she had taken it off to wash her hands, in the bathroom of a store we had visited earlier that day. A quick phone call revealed the business was closed. We then began to verbally retrace our steps, so that I could begin my phone calling and searching at first light. But Deb found no solace in my plan, and we systematically began to dismantle the motel room, piece by piece, searching every possible hiding place. We also alerted the motel staff, in case some kind soul might find it and turn it in.

"Maybe it fell behind the TV", she suggested.

"We've already looked there...twice. Actually, we've already looked everywhere there is to look."

"We'll let's look again." She would not be deterred.

The Television was sitting on a simple, faux-wood. table-like affair, with six to eight inches, sticking out on each side of the TV. I had already picked up the Television off the stand, and set it aside; then moved the table away from the wall, turned it upside down, and searched through the accumulated stuff the cleaning people never see, in search of the missing treasure. Now we repeated the whole process again. I could already see there would be no rest for the weary on this night. And furthermore, it was our long-anticipated wedding anniversary trip, and rather than a celebratory mood, I found myself trying, in vain, to console my weeping, heart-broken bride.

With Debbie finally convinced that the ring could not possibly be anywhere in our room, and after having her see for herself (again) on and around the television, I placed the TV back on its stand, and wiped the spider webs from my hands onto my jeans.

"I'll never find it, and we can't afford another one", she sobbed, as she headed back to the bathroom to remove the makeup the tears had not already washed away.

Take it to the Lord, in Prayer

"Hold on a minute", I said, "we haven't really prayed about it. Let's stop now and ask the Lord to help us find it."

She heartily agreed, and we held hands and knelt beside the bed to commit the matter to prayer. And pray we did, reminding the Lord that He knew exactly where that ring was at that very moment, even though we did not. We also "advised" Him that if someone had picked it up, He should motivate them to turn it in, so I could find it the next day, when I went back to retrace our steps.

Still sniffling, Deb returned to her makeup removal, and I decided to try to find the baseball game again. Both of us continued silently calling out to the Lord to restore the lost ring – me from the easy chair, and her from the bathroom.

An Unforgettable Answer

Just as I found the station, she stuck her head out of the bathroom to remind me of another place we should put on our list to include in our search the next day. Then all of a sudden I heard a scream that made the hair stand up on my neck.

"WHERE DID YOU FIND IT!?!?!?"

I jumped up, as if I'd been shot out of a cannon, and ran to where she was standing. "Find what?" This was getting ridiculous.

"My ring… where did you find it, and why didn't you tell me?

Her eyes were locked in a fixed gaze, staring like she was mesmerized, at the space on the television stand, just next to the TV set. I was on the other side of the TV stand, and thought she must have been joking, even though this was no joking matter. I cautiously walked over to where she was standing, still staring, and there it was! Her ring was right there on the top of the TV table, in full view, glistening like the full moon on an October night. It was sitting there in the open space, on the stand, beside the television. The same television I had picked up and moved, and the same stand I had turned upside down and looked under. This was not possible.

She did not move or blink, but repeated her question, as if transfixed, "Where did you find it?"

"Honey… I did not find it", I stammered, not knowing what to say. "I *promise* I don't know where it came from." Now my gaze was fixed on the shiny object, and I must have sounded like I'd seen a ghost.

Suddenly we were both covered in goosebumps. I had personally removed the television three times, leaving the bare stand exposed. There was no possible way under heaven, we could have missed seeing the ring. We had searched every nook and cranny in that tiny room, and the TV stand was the most noticeable, visible thing in the whole place. At that moment, we knew God had miraculously answered our prayer, and returned the ring, from wherever it had been lost.

"How do you suppose it got there,?" Debbie asked.

Then it hit us both, like a ton of bricks.

"**HE** brought it here, didn't He?" we whispered, almost in unison.

"That must mean He was here, in this very room," I added.

Once we realized what we had witnessed, we returned to our knees for a time of thanksgiving and worship, like we've never experienced before or since. I don't know why He did it, but we both knew we had received a personal visitation from God – or an angel

He had dispatched. Even though He has a universe to rule over, our loving Heavenly Father took time to allay the heartbreak of a wife who lost a sentimental treasure, and a husband who desperately realized he had no way to "fix" the situation. To this day, when we find ourselves facing seemingly impossible circumstances, one of us usually reminds the other to remember "the ring". That anniversary turned out to be our best ever, as we were reminded, in a very unusual way, that God truly knows and cares – about everything in our lives. And He can even choose to make "house calls" if He takes a notion. "For with God, nothing shall be impossible". (Luke 1:37 KJV)

★★★

PUTTING A HANDLE ON IT...

1) *Times of Refreshing.*

I mentioned that Debbie and I used the motorcycle as our way of getting away, and taking a break. Understanding that everyone needs a break occasionally, what things refresh and renew you? _____

_____

Jesus spoke to His disciples about getting away for a time of rest (Mark 6:35) If it was necessary for them, isn't it for us as well? Someone much wiser than me said, we should "divert daily, withdraw weekly, and abandon annually". None of us are invincible, and God's principles of the Sabbath and the Sabbatical are included in His Word for a reason.

2) <u>*Modern Day Miracles*</u>

Do you believe God still performs miracles today? (Yes / No / Maybe) Why or why not?

_____

We know from a multitude of Scriptural references, that God is a miracle-working God. We also know that one of His attributes is that of Immutability, meaning He is unchanging and unchangeable (Malachi 3:6). In other words, the same God Whose miracles are seen in the lives of Moses, Daniel, David, etc., is the God we worship and serve today. And furthermore, since He does not change, there is no reason to doubt that He cannot miraculously act on our behalf, if He chooses to do so today. Sure, there are a lot of shenanigans today, in the name of miracles and wonders, but God is still God, His power has not diminished, and nothing is impossible for Him (Luke 1:37). We cannot "throw the baby out with the bathwater", just because there are crooked sensationalists, duping ignorant people for financial gain. Let's not let them ruin it for those who truly want to believe the God of the Bible.

3) *Lost and Found*

Have you ever lost something that was really important to you, and felt desperate to find it? (Yes / No) I wonder if you've considered that God has never lost anything. 2 Chronicles reminds us that "The eyes of the Lord run to and fro throughout the whole earth..." (KJV) He sees every inch of His creation at any moment. Nothing is hidden to Him. And if He can see tiny objects on His planet, making Google Earth seem as outdated as an 8 track tape, does that not mean He sees us as well? The Psalmist certainly thought so. Read for yourself his thoughts on this subject, as recorded in Psalm 34:15, and most of Psalm 139.

4) *The Doctor Is In*

Think of, and list at least one specific way in which you need God to show up in your life right now. _____

_____

Obviously, we cannot put God in a box, or orchestrate how He will act, but we can call out to Him in time of need (Jeremiah 33:3), and let Him decide the best course of action to meet our needs. Debbie and I simply asked God to allow us to find the ring, but He chose to do exceeding, abundantly, above all we asked or thought (Ephesians 3:20). Go to Him, sincerely and fervently, with your needs, and then worship and thank Him for the way He chooses to respond. He is God, and He knows what is best in every situation. And sometimes He may choose to surprise the socks off of us. When He does, remember, that's not odd....that's God!

Chapter Eight

BRADLEY'S HOPE

(Matthew 25:40)

Ministry in Jesus' Name

During the years in which I served as the pastor of a small church, near Savannah, GA, my wife, Debbie, enjoyed volunteering at the nursing home down the street. She would go room to room, encouraging the patients, sharing the love of Christ, reading Bible portions to them, praying for them, helping to meet personal needs, etc. The patients there became like family to her, and she took a personal interest in them, learning about their relatives, their life stories, their needs, likes and dislikes, etc. She would ask specific questions, Debbie came to be on a first-name basis with the nurses and staff, and was often "accosted" when she walked in the door, with requests and suggestions, regarding which patients were having a bad day, or could most use her ministry at that particular time. Through her genuine way of sharing the love of God, a number of the residents came to faith in Christ, and several of the staff eventually became active members of our church. She says she even put our Irish Terrier, Rose, "into the ministry," by bringing her along to help minister to the patients, as a therapy dog.

On one particular day, after a long afternoon of ministering to needy people, Debbie was about to leave the nursing home, when she noticed a couple of people she had not seen there before. They had come from a neighboring state, to visit one of the residents. And the young man they had come to see was a patient with which Debbie had not yet become acquainted. Because she had been there awhile, and was on her way out the door, she did not stay and talk to them for long. But in her customary way, she did hand the couple a Gospel tract, and asked them the question, "Has anyone told you today, that Jesus loves you?" She then headed home to prepare supper for her waiting husband.

A couple of weeks passed, and Debbie received an unusual phone call. The couple she had given the tract to, called to ask if they could come by our house and speak with her in person. They had traced Deb down from the information printed on the back of the tract. They did not indicate why they wanted to see her, but Debbie agreed to meet with them, and an appointment was arranged.

Dave and Judy were family friends, of the young man they had been visiting in the nursing home that day. They were impressed with Debbie's genuine love for the Lord, and eagerness to share Him with people, others seem to have forgotten. So they decided to come get better acquainted with her, and to share some of Bradley's story. As it turned out, his family all lived in another part of the country, and were only able to have very limited contact with him. So this couple would drive an hour or so from their home in a neighboring state, to see that Bradley received an occasional visit, from someone he knew. But his condition kept them from feeling like their visits were meaningful or effective. Therefore, they had an offer to make. In order to assure that Bradley received regular visits, they wanted to pay Debbie to visit him each week, and try to read the Bible to him.

Deb immediately responded that her ministry to the patients in the nursing home, was a ministry of love, and that although their offer was generous and appreciated, she would not accept financial remuneration for what she did. She said her philosophy of ministry was taken from the Scripture in which Jesus instructed His disciples with these words: "freely you have received; freely give" (Matthew 10:8). However, she did agree to add the young man to the list of people she would see during her nursing home visits. What she didn't tell them was that Bradley's type actually scared her, and she had no idea how she would communicate with him. But she was willing to give it a try. That's when Dave and Judy began to share some of Bradley's sad story with Deb, in order for her to know what she was getting herself into.

A man with many needs

While in his early thirties, and enlisted in the U.S. Navy, apparently Bradley had made some very poor choices during a shore leave, resulting in a drug overdose, which led to a major, debilitating stroke. The stroke left him little more than a quadriplegic - unable to speak, swallow, or use his arms and legs. Over the next few years, his atrophied body became practically useless, but his mind remained sharp and clear. Realizing he was a prisoner in his own body, and given little to no promise of improvement, Bradley became angry, bitter, and hopeless, often despairing of life. He would not be easy to visit or minister to, but Debbie agreed to see what she could do. Because Bradley had no family living in the area, and with his bleak prognosis, he had been assigned to hospice care, with the code DNR (do not resuscitate) on his medical chart. He was basically left to die.

The next time she went to make her visits, Debbie spent extra time in the car, asking God for grace and wisdom to know how to minister to the very needy young man. She went in, and found his room. Gulping hard she entered, and introduced herself to the patient with her usual, "Hello Bradley, I'm Debbie. Has anyone told you today, that Jesus loves you?" He turned his head toward the wall, as if to ignore her, in hopes she would leave him alone, and go bother someone else. She tried to encourage him the best she could, shared a few verses of Scripture and prayed with him, receiving little response. Deb was not used to being ignored, and decided to accept the challenge of winning Bradley over, by God's grace, and with His help.

She continued stopping by his room, even though his response changed very little, at first. But as the visits continued, Bradley began slowly showing signs of warming up to her, and God began to put a special burden in Deb's heart for the sad and lonely young man.

Breakthrough!

Because of Bradley's inability to speak, or use his hands, communicating with him was nigh unto impossible. Without some way of knowing what he was thinking, it was very difficult to know if anything Debbie shared with him was penetrating his mind and heart. So she came up with the idea of preparing a white board, with the letters of the alphabet, numbers, etc., written in large print. For the next few months, Debbie and Bradley developed a laborious system of questions and answers. She learned many things about him, his family, his likes, dislikes, etc. She would ask specific questions, then point to the board, with Bradley nodding or blinking when the right letter or number was selected. She would then put the letters together to form words, and the words together to form sentences. As they perfected their special means of "talking" together, Debbie and Bradley slowly became "buds". For her, it was a way to learn about this interesting young man, who had so much to share, but had not had a way to do so. For Bradley, there was now an opportunity to get outside himself, and explain details of his life that had long been locked up tight. A whole new world was about to open to him...to them both. After utilizing their special communication method for countless hours, Deb was able to piece together bits of information about Bradley's family; including each members' name, age, birthday, etc. She also learned about his past, his hobbies, his fears, dreams, accomplishments, etc. She discovered that he had been a concert pianist, who also played guitar, as well as several other instruments. She found out he was a sports enthusiast, and learned the names of his favorite teams in each sport. In addition, she was able to find out about when and where he was hurting, if he needed or wanted anything, required medical attention, etc. She came to know his situation almost better than the medical staff in charge of his care. Armed with this helpful information, Debbie could insure Bradley was given the best possible care by the facility employees.

Deb began to help her friend with some of his personal needs, like clipping his fingernails, moisturizing his throat with swabs, and applying lip balm to his cracked lips. Because he could not swallow, his mouth and throat were constantly dry and parched, so her visits brought him much needed physical relief, as well as encouragement. The medical staff began being more attentive to him when Debbie was not there, because they knew she would be checking on him regularly; and not only that, he was now able to tell her things which he had been unable to communicate, previously. She became his advocate, and he now anxiously looked forward to her visits. Often, before leaving his room, Debbie would take the young man's withered hand and pray with him, only to have him grip as hard as he could squeeze, doing his best to keep her from departing.

Now that Debbie had developed a growing relationship with Bradley, and had learned to communicate with him, she began to zero in on his spiritual needs. These visits always included the reading of Scripture and prayer, but it was more tolerated than enjoyed by Bradley. He truly appreciated Debbie's ministry to him, but had no particular interest in the things of the Lord. One day, during one of their visits, Debbie felt led to read Isaiah 53. Bradley laid there in his usual ho-hum way, until he heard the prophetic words about Jesus being described as "despised and rejected of men; a man of sorrows, and acquainted with grief." Suddenly Bradley's eyes widened, and he began to stare at Deb, as if drinking in every word. Noticing his change in disposition, she went on to carefully explain the passage. It was evident that the broken, hopeless young man was drawn to the Savior, as He was presented by the ancient prophet Isaiah. He had heard of Jesus, but had never thought of Him in this light. A Man of sorrows? Bradley understood that. Acquainted with grief? He knew about that as well. Despised and rejected? Those were also terms with which he was familiar. His demeanor suggested that he wanted to learn more about this One with Whom he could so readily identify. Debbie lovingly explained why Jesus' love for us, motivated

Him to go through these things; and that because He did, we now have the opportunity of receiving the eternal life He offers, to broken, sinful people.

Deb asked Bradley if he would like to invite Jesus to enter his life, making him a new creature, and guaranteeing him a home in heaven. The young man eagerly expressed his desire in the affirmative, and she patiently helped him formulate a prayer to the Lord, stating his desire. Debbie did not walk out of that room that day; she *floated* out, and hurried home to tell me of our new brother in Christ.

He ain't heavy, he's my brother!

As the visits continued, Bradley began expressing a keen desire to learn the Bible, and usually could not get enough of being read to. And not only did he listen with new interest, the truths were sinking in. It was obvious that Bradley was extremely bright, and seldom did Debbie quiz him over the materials they read or studied, that he failed to answer each question perfectly. One habit they developed, became especially meaningful to Deb. Often during their visits, she would ask, "Bradley, where is Jesus right now?" He would then begin to very, very slowly and laboriously raise his withered, atrophied arm up, up, up, until it pointed skyward, indicating Jesus was in Heaven. She would then ask, "and where *else* is Jesus?" At which time he would carefully lower his hand down, until it rested on his chest, just over his heart.

Over the course of Debbie's visits with Bradley, those responsible for his medical and physical care, as well as some of his family members, noticed a new attitude of hope in him, which had not been evident previously. No longer did he long for death, but now wanted to live, and even caused them to wonder if he might be able to make some physical improvements with proper help. It soon became apparent that he might even be a candidate for some forms of therapy and/or rehabilitation.

Bradley's loving sister, Kim, who lived in Pennsylvania, grieved the fact that she was so far from her brother, and unable to be more involved in his life. The distance prohibited more than a few visits a year, and she longed to have him closer to her family, so they could be there for him. So through much perseverance, and seemingly endless paperwork, phone calls, etc., she was able to arrange for him to be moved to a good facility near her home. There she would become his caregiver, and arrange for the help that might improve his life. However, Kim was unaware of the relationship that had developed between Bradley and Debbie, or even that Debbie had been visiting him. She didn't even know there was a Debbie involved in her brother's life.

<u>Gone!</u>

On the other hand, Debbie knew all about Kim, through her "talks" with Bradley. She had also caught snippets of information, indicating he might be moved to another facility, but knew nothing of the details. Deb was excited for the possibility of Bradley being able to be closer to caring family members, but knew his moving would create a great void in her life. Not only had she invested heavily into his life, but he had become a great source of blessing and inspiration to her as well. Because Kim had no knowledge of Debbie, she arranged for the move to take place without Debbie's knowledge. Even Bradley was unaware of the impending move until just before it took place, so he could not inform Debbie. Needless to say, she was crushed one day to simply show up for a visit, only to learn he was gone. Two years and three months of pouring her life into his, and she was not even able to tell him goodbye. Not only that, because of the HIPPA laws, no one in the nursing home would or could give Debbie information about where Bradley had gone. To say she was devastated would be a gross understatement.

Thankfully, from her visits with Bradley, Deb knew the general area where Kim lived, and through some digging, and phone calling she was able to finally discover that her friend had been placed in a facility located in central Pennsylvania. She obtained the address and wrote him, but had no way to know if he was even receiving her letters. One day she finally made contact with Bradley's new facility. She spoke to a nurse, and asked that her phone number be given to one of his family members, with the request that they give her a call.

A few days later the call finally came from Kim, and Debbie was excited to learn of Bradley's improving status, and to talk to the sister he had told her so much about. During the conversation, Debbie inquired about several of the other family members, including Kim's children. Kim immediately became very suspicious, and finally asked, "How in the world do you know so much about our family?" Deb quickly replied, "Bradley told me about them." Now Kim was really skeptical, and shot back, "What do you mean Bradley told you? He can't even talk." Debbie then began to explain about her visits with her favorite patient, and their special method of communication. Kim was overwhelmed. She did not even know that Bradley had been receiving regular visits, much less the care and attention Deb had given him. The call ended with Kim inviting Debbie to come visit Bradley, and meet the rest of the family in person. Deb shared with me about the conversation, and asked me if I had ever heard of the small town where Kim lived.

"Negative."

But a quick internet search revealed something very interesting. Bradley had been moved to a suburb of Harrisburg, PA, which happens to be the very city in which Debbie was born (although she had grown up in south Florida). Debbie had been wanting us to visit there for nearly 30 years, but we had never been able to work it out. In addition, Debbie had also been talking about Bradley's upcoming birthday, and bemoaning the fact that she would not be able to visit him on that day, as she had done for the past few years. The same week all of this was occurring, the church I was pastoring, unexpectedly gave the two of us a monetary gift for our birthdays, which are both in March. So I hatched a plan.

I checked mileages, made reservations, and told Debbie I knew how I wanted to spend my part of our birthday money – I wanted to take her to visit Harrisburg, and see Bradley. She was ecstatic. We arrived late on Sunday night, after a long 13 hour drive. Exhausted, we slept in a little the next morning, but were on our way to the nursing home around mid morning. We had informed Kim of our coming, but told her to keep it a secret from Bradley.

Glad Reunion

The look on his face when Debbie stepped into his room was priceless. This was the birthday present he never expected to receive. We visited him that day until he began to grow tired, and then left so he could rest. We spent the middle of the day looking around the town, and finding some of the familiar sights Deb remembered from her early childhood. We then returned in the afternoon, for another visit. Debbie was thrilled to see the improvements Bradley had made since being moved to this new facility. Therapy had begun, and progress was evident in several areas of his life. He was also being "fitted" for a special computer, which might eventually enable him to communicate via e-mail, etc.

As the time approached for us to say our "good byes", and our visit with Bradley was coming to a close, Debbie couldn't resist the urge to ask one more time, "Bradley, where is Jesus?". Slowly and resolutely, his arm began its familiar upward motion, until it was pointing Heavenward. She then asked him the second part, and we watched as his hand came to rest on his chest. In his tedious, determined way, his answer indicated, that although Bradley had now moved far away from us, Jesus was still right there with him. His eternal hope was still alive and well.

★★

PUTTING A HANDLE ON IT:

1) *The Least of These*

Why do you think some Christians feel uncomfortable ministering to people who are less fortunate than they are? _____

_____

When we struggle to provide ministry to these people, we should consider the fact that, the tables could easily be turned. We could be the ones in need of someone to care for us, rather than the ones given the opportunity to care for others. Read, and then write out Mark 10:45. _____

_____

Throughout the New Testament, what attitudes did Jesus demonstrate toward others – especially those who had serious problems? List some of His attitudes here: _____

_____

2) *They Are Precious in His Sight*

We all know we should not "judge a book by its cover", but it is easy to do, isn't it? Society often writes people off who have handicaps or infirmities, thinking them to be of less value than "normal" people. Does God view some people as more, or less valuable than others? _____ Notice what Jesus taught about ministering to "the least of these"? (Matthew 25:31-45)

3) *Here Am I, Send Me*

Who do you know of, less fortunate than yourself, that could probably use some personal ministry this week? _____ Think of some practical ways you might go about it. Send a card? Make a personal visit? Read to them? You don't have to have special training to care for others.

Take a moment to consider this thought….Someone in history, is quoted to have uttered the famous words, <u>*"It is more blessed to give than to receive."*</u> We generally think that the opposite is true. However, *if* the person making that statement had never personally given anything of much significance, then we can write it off as journalistic hype. But, on the other hand, if the one making that statement had really given anything of great value, we would have to consider the source, and believe they might be on to an important truth. Look up Acts 20:35, and notice who is stated to have made that declaration. Then write the name here: _____ How should this affect our view of the statement?

_____

Ask the Lord who He would have you to give yourself to, in loving ministry, during the next few weeks. Ask him to reveal someone who is incapable of paying you back. Then determine to treat them, in the same way you would want to be treated, if it were you, in need of a loving touch, helping hand, or listening ear. And when you do this, be mindful, of who seems to be receiving the greatest blessing.

Chapter Nine

DEB'S DIVINE DECORATOR

(Proverbs 8:20, 21; Matthew 6:33)

"...rise up, and call her blessed"

My dear wife, Debbie, is one of the most frugal as well as practical people I know. During our more than three decades of full-time ministry, she has chosen (with my blessing) to remain a stay-at-home mom and wife. I've never had a large salary, so we have learned to "make do" with what we have had, and Deb has become the world's best improviser. For years, she was the family barber, even cutting her own hair. I only sat in her chair once, but she said I was too squirmy and picky, so my free haircut days totaled only one. My bad. She taught herself to sew, and made beautiful dresses for herself and for our girls; as well as curtains, pillow shams, etc. We did eat out occasionally, but usually suppertime found our family sitting around the table at home, enjoying one of Debbie's delicious recipes.

But her gift for improvising was often really demonstrated when it came to decorating the house. She found ways to make things match, to put items together which other people might not think about. With her touch, our house was always neat, attractive, and spotlessly clean. She had a knack for taking random things people gave us, and adding them to the décor as if she had planned it that way from the outset. She would often be heard to say, as she stood back and admired a new arrangement or ensemble, "See, God is my Divine Decorator. He gives us the items He wants us to use, then tells me how to arrange them." Hey, it works for me.

Matches made in Heaven

One day, during a visit to our house, by our son, Nathan and his sweet wife, Kate (plus their ever-present Winston the Westie), Deb was given a lovely shower curtain, which they had recently "retired", and replaced with another design. Though the curtain was pretty - sort of a mixed floral print, with flowers I could not identify, I couldn't see it matching anything we had, and wondered what she would do with it. I sort of expected her to tell them she couldn't use it. Nevertheless, at the end of the visit, Nate, Kate, and Sir Winston headed back to Charlotte, and the curtain remained in Chatham County, GA. Sure enough, a few weeks later, I came home to find it hanging in the guest bathroom, accessorized in such a way that one would swear it was all thought out in advance, and purchased together as an ensemble.

Some months later, we received a visit from a friend who had spent some time in the Orient. He brought us a souvenir in the form of a simple, hand-painted picture, purchased from a sidewalk vendor. It almost resembled a scroll, measuring approximately 14" X 20", and contained a sketchy picture of some kind of small bird, sitting on a fence, next to a group of large flowering plants. It also contained some Oriental writing, which our friend said was a Bible verse – 1st Peter 5:7, "Casting all your care on Him, for He careth for you."

It was an attractive piece, but different in design and makeup, from anything else we had in the house. Though Debbie was very creative in using things which came into our possession, not everything made it on the wall, or in the living area of our home. Our attic contained a few boxes of things that just didn't fit. I fully expected this painting to end up in this category, joining other nice, but unused items we had acquired along life's journey - things we did not want to get rid of, but never quite found a place for. However, for some reason, the unusual painting remained in the house, and not in the attic, while Debbie tried to understand what she might do with it.

"I've been wanting something for this space for awhile. Would you hold this picture here, and let me see what I think?" she asked me one day, indicating a spot on the living room wall. Our house was a split floor plan, with the Master bedroom and bath on one end; the living room, dining room and kitchen in the middle; and two bedrooms on the other end, with a bathroom in between. Just to the right of the doorway, leading into the guest bath and two bedrooms, was single straight-backed chair against the wall, facing into the living room. The place she was pointing to was a blank space on the wall just above the chair. The colors on the painting were in the same family as the living room furniture, and the picture did seem to fit well in the chosen space, although it was different in nature and design, than anything else we had in that room. After having me hold it while she stood back and studied it, Deb decided it was a "go". A little centering, a little hammering, some more looking, and there it hung, seeming to fit right in.

For the next day or so, every time I walked by the new picture, something about it caught my attention, but I just couldn't put my finger on what it was. One day as I stood, staring at the painting, trying to figure out what drew me to it, my eyes wandered from the print, into the narrow hallway to its left, and then through the opened door of the guest bathroom. That's when it hit me.

"Debbie, can you come here a minute?" I called excitedly. "You're not going to believe this."

"What is it?" she asked as she entered the living room wiping her hands on a dish towel.

"Stand back here and look at that picture you hung on the wall. Tell me what you see."

"Why, is something wrong with it? Is it crooked?"

"No, nothing like that. Keep looking."

"I don't know what you're getting at. It looks fine to me."

"Sure it looks fine. But look just to the left of it, into the bathroom. The flowers on the painting are identical to the little flowers on the shower curtain Kate gave us. They're a perfect match."

"Well, what do you know?" she smiled with satisfaction, "I had not noticed that before. It just goes to show that My Divine Decorator has been at it again."

★★★

PUTTING A HANDLE ON IT:

1) *The God of Beauty and Detail*

Have you ever thought of our Creator God as a Divine Decorator? After all, is not He the One Who designed and created all that is good and wonderful in this world? According to the Book of Genesis, He spoke into existence the cardinal and the cheetah; the North Star and Niagara Falls; the daffodil and the mourning dove.

Understanding that everyone has different tastes, list three or four things, in God's creation, which you find to be beautiful. _____

_____

2) *The God Who Cares About the Small Stuff*

We may have had meager resources for decorating our house, but as we served and depended on the Lord, He always seemed to find a way to show He cared – even about a faithful wife wanting her décor to match. What is a need or desire in your life, you might have considered too small, to warrant God's attention? _____

I love the old camp song we used to sing, which says,

> *"How big is God! How big and wide His vast domain;*
> *To try to tell, these lips can only start.*
> *He's big enough to rule this mighty universe,*
> *Yet small enough to live within my heart."*

Don't ever think the small things which you care about, don't matter to God.

3) *Devine Designer*

I am continually amazed at the way God orchestrates things in our lives. In the case of this story, it was bringing a sidewalk painting from the other side of the world, and a shower curtain from Charlotte, NC, to hang together in a house in Chatham County, GA. The God Who causes the galaxies to soar through the heavens in perfect synchronization, has the ability, wisdom, and desire to orchestrate the events of your life; when it is for your good, and His glory. We must not limit what our Devine Designer can do.

Can you think of a circumstance or situation, in which God supernaturally brought some things together, which would not have happened otherwise? (an unexpected meeting with someone; a tool you found which you later used to fix something; a matching outfit which you needed for a particular occasion, etc.) _____

_____

Learn to put 1st Peter 5:7 to work in your life. He wants us to cast all of our cares on Him, because He really does care for us. What is one heavy burden you know you need to "cast on Him" this week? _____

Why not practice what this verse says, concerning your particular care, and see how the Divine Designer might choose to orchestrate things in your world, to demonstrate His care for you?

Chapter Ten

INTERSTATE INTERVENTION

(Psalm 91:11; Isaiah 54:17)

Each of the stories in this book have to do with God's providence in our lives. I'm convinced that the providence of God is much more active and frequent than we realize, and when we find ourselves in eternity, we will see just how much God really was involved in our lives, here on earth. Sometimes His activity is hidden, and happens without our recognition or knowledge. Other times, His Divine intervention is more pronounced, making it difficult, if not impossible to miss. This story speaks of the latter.

Life is a vapor

Debbie and I had just finished paying our respects, at the public viewing of a friend who had died, and were on our way back home. My parents, in their 80's at the time, had planned to go with us, but backed out at the last minute. They agreed, instead, to wait at home, and go out with us to supper, once we returned from the time of visitation. The afternoon viewing was in Savannah, roughly 15-20 miles from Pooler, where we lived. By the time we were headed back home, rush hour had hit… and hit with a vengeance. As we made our way along I-16 Westbound, in our 2000 Honda Civic, I was already thinking about what I might have for supper, since our destination was to be Fordham's Farmhouse Restaurant, in Statesboro, one of my favorites.

Smashed!

We were moving along at around 55-60 mph, with heavy traffic all around us, so I chose to remain in the right lane, chatting with Deb about everything in general, and nothing in particular. The lane immediately to our left was open, and I thought nothing of the eighteen-wheeled log truck I saw coming up from our rear, about to pass me on the left. Then all of a sudden, without warning, the sound of screeching tires and crunching metal, drowned out our conversation, and in the next split second, we realized it was *our tires and our metal.* Just as the truck's nose pulled even with our car's back door, the driver unexpectedly decided to switch into the right lane. The only problem was that we happened to be there. As the right front corner of his bumper slammed into the left quarter panel of our little civic, the impact instantly shoved the rear of our little car to the right, simultaneously causing the front end to violently jerk to the left. But rather than back off after hitting us, the trucker kept on pushing through to our lane, as if trying to ram us off the road. As the front end of our car lunged left, the nose of the heavy truck struck it as well. This second hit (which almost seemed like one continuous collision) catapulted the front end of our vehicle back to the right, sending our little car spinning out of control, like a whirling dervish. Round and round we went, in a clockwise motion, with the momentum carrying us off the interstate and onto the right shoulder of the road. But the horrible impact had been so great, that the spinning continued, like a rogue tornado, we spun in a huge arc-like motion, from the shoulder of the road, and right back onto I-16, into the lanes of rushing traffic.

This instantly set in motion a jumbled mess of swerving, braking and screeching, by the cars behind and around us, in an effort to miss the little car gyrating across the packed lanes of traffic. With each revolution, Deb and I were being snapped back and forth, like being in a carnival ride on steroids. Still spinning, round and round, we spun all the way across both lanes of traffic and finally stopped spinning only as we slammed into the guard rail, in the median of the interstate. But although the spinning stopped, the sliding did not. Now we were smashed against the guard rail, facing backwards toward the oncoming traffic, with the force of the impact still pushing the car down the road. Pinned against the railing like it was magnetized, we slid backwards another 100 yards, before coming to a stop. Smoke and the smell of burning rubber filled the car. Rush hour drivers who had been dodging us and each other, like sparks flying out of a crackling campfire, now started pulling over and exiting their cars. The noise during the spinning and the sliding was deafening; then as suddenly as it started, there was total silence.

I took a deep breath and looked over at Debbie. "Are you okay?" I quickly asked, immediately thankful that we had, merely seconds before the collision, remembered to fasten our seat belts. I knew she was still in the car, and still alive because her screaming didn't stop until the car finally did.

"I...I... think so. What about you?"

"I believe I'm fine, but we need to get out of the car before it explodes", was my concern.

Her door was smashed shut from slamming into, and sliding along the guard rail. And though my side had taken the brunt of the impact, I managed to kick, what was left of the driver's door open. Both sides of the vehicle had sustained major damage, so it was a wonder either door opened. Making our way out of the mangled car, we stumbled down the median, for 50 yards or so, to be a safe distance away in the event of an explosion or fire. Once we were clear of the wreck, and our hearts settled down a bit, we took inventory of each other, to make sure we were both all there. With great amazement and gratefulness to the Lord, we realized neither of us had received as much as a scratch.

People were now getting out of their cars and running toward the mangled Honda. Only by God's grace, no other cars were hit, or hit each other in the melee. One man saw us standing there and said to me, "Can you come and help me check on the people in that little car? I don't know if they're even alive, but would you come with me, to see about them?"

"Sir, we _ARE_ the people from that car", I answered.

"No way...that's not possible! You're not even bleeding." He was dumbfounded. "I was following your car, and the whole thing looked like something from the NASCAR highlight reel. Cars were swerving all over the interstate to keep from getting hit. I've never seen anything like it. Do you realize how lucky you are?"

"God is good, and we know He protected us", we answered.

Seven or eight cars back, in the traffic behind us, making his way home from work, was a policeman who had formerly attended our church. He kindly and graciously tended to us, and stayed with us until help arrived. Also, sitting stuck in the unmoving traffic which had backed up on the interstate, was my brother, Kevin, trying to make his way home from work. Of course he was unaware that the reason for his being stuck there, was me. I called his cell phone, and told him what had happened. Once he could make his way to the accident scene, he gave us a lift to our house, as the wrecker hauled our mangled car away. The driver of the log truck didn't even slow down, and was never apprehended.

Debbie and I have no doubt at all, that God's protective hand was with us in that car. If we ever witnessed an obvious display of His providence, it was then. We also know we could have very easily entered eternity during that accident. To this day, we both realize our Heavenly Father must have had a reason for keeping us around a little longer. Since that event, we look at life differently, knowing very vividly, how quickly it can be taken away. Now we want to live each day for His glory, seeking to do His will, for the remainder of our time on this earth.

"Only one life, so soon 'twill be past; only what's done for Christ will last."

★★

PUTTING A HANDLE ON IT:

1) *The Protective Hand of God*

Can you think of a time, when you knew, beyond a shadow of a doubt, that God supernaturally protected you? If so, write a short version of the event, and any pertinent facts here:

_____

_____

_____

_____

Only in eternity, will we probably understand the numbers of times God has Divinely spared us from injury, disease, or death. For every time we're aware of, there are probably many numbers of times we did not know about. The late Dr. Jerry Falwell, paraphrasing Isaiah 54:17, was often heard to say, "The person of God is indestructible until God is through with him/her." He believed, and lived like he believed, that nothing could take the servant of God out, until their "appointed time" to die. They are actually invincible until they have finished the tasks God put them on earth to do. So, we should not live with fear or worry about what might happen to us, but serve God boldly and confidently each day.

Write down something you've spent time and energy worrying about, within the past six months, which never occurred. _____

_____

Its been said that 95% of the things we spend time worrying about never come to pass. Read Philippians 4:6, then write out a paraphrase of it, in your own words: _____

_____

_____

2) *We All Have an Appointment We Will Keep*

Having mentioned God's protective hand, we must also consider that the Bible says, "It is appointed unto man once to die, and after this, the judgment." (KJV Hebrews 9:27) Each of us does have a pre-determined appointment with death, which we will keep, unless we are fortunate enough to be included in the Rapture. And the other side of the coin, is that none of us knows exactly when that set appointment is. Debbie and I, by all human standards, should have entered eternity on that fateful day in April 2011. But obviously, the time had not come for our appointment. We are confident that God spared our lives, because He isn't finished with us yet. Therefore, we should live each day as if it will be our last…because one day it will be.

What is one thing you would definitely do today, if God supernaturally revealed that it would be your last day on earth? _____

How do you know it won't be?

3) *He Knows What We Need, Even When We Don't*

Our little Honda was pushing 150,000 miles on the odometer, and we knew it would soon need some major mechanical attention. Although it is a rough way to replace a vehicle, through the wreck, and the insurance adjustment, plus an unexpected gift, we were able to purchase a much better, nicer, and more dependable car than the one we were driving. We were unaware that the next phase of our lives would require numbers of lengthy road trips, which our Civic may not have been able to withstand. We were not in the position to buy another car, but in His grace and mercy, God gave us the vehicle He knew we would need in the coming days. When unexpected problems come into your life, understand that God has not lost control, nor ceased to care for you. He often uses trials and difficulties to bring about a better plan – one we might not have considered, had it not been for the problems He allowed.

THE JOURNEY CONTINUES...

So there you have it. Ten different stories, from Debbie's and my life and ministry, which reflect the evidence of God's Divine providence. And these are not nearly all we could share... there are lots more. I just selected a few of our favorites to share at this time.

Over the years, as I have related our stories to others, I've occasionally been accused of being a mystic. I really did not know whether to be offended or flattered, until recently, when I looked up the definition in the dictionary. My copy of Webster's dictionary defines mysticism as, "belief in the possibility of attaining direct communication with God; or having knowledge of spiritual truths...." I guess if that is what it means, I would have to plead "guilty" as charged.

You see, I happen to believe God's Word to be totally true, dependable, and infallible - from cover to cover. And as the old country preacher said, "I even believe the cover; because it says Holy Bible." In my Bible, God invites me to come boldly before His throne of grace, to bring my needs directly to Him in prayer (Hebrews 4:16). That sounds like an invitation for communication to me. In Jeremiah 33:3, God says for His followers to "call upon Him...", more communication. In Romans 5:1,2, the Apostle Paul reminds me that through a personal relationship with Jesus Christ, I now have access to God, the Father. As a matter of fact, the Bible is filled with, not only God's invitations to talk to Him in prayer, but many examples demonstrating that it is His desire to communicate directly with the human element of His creation.

You or I would be thrown in jail so fast it would make us dizzy, if we tried to walk through the doors of the White House, and attempted to approach the President, in order to speak to him. Yet, through Christ, I can personally address the eternal, almighty, sovereign God anytime I choose to do so. That's some pretty heavy communication.

Second, a mystic is one who believes he can have knowledge of Spiritual truths. Unless I'm sadly mistaken, one of the primary functions of the Holy Spirit, which indwells every believer, is to teach us spiritual truth, as we read and study God's Word. The Bible contains all the spiritual truth we'll ever need, and it encourages us to drink deeply of its contents; feeding our souls, and growing in our knowledge of its timeless truths. Throughout the Bible we are admonished to read God's Word, study God's Word, meditate on God's Word, memorize God's Word, etc. So if a mystic is one who believes God is a God who wants us to personally communicate with Him, and Him with us; *and* that it is possible to know and understand spiritual truths, I'll gladly wear that title. I am so very grateful our Heavenly

Father is One with Whom we can commune on a daily basis, and One about Whom we can continue to learn as long as we live.

So how about you, dear reader? Are you a mystic (according to Mr. Webster)? Do you believe you can personally communicate with God, and know Spiritual truth? Jesus stated that one of the reasons He came to this earth, was so that mankind could "have life, and have it more abundantly" (John 10:10). Through genuine faith in His death, burial, and resurrection, which was provided to pay the price of our sins, we can enter into an eternal relationship with Him. The ongoing results of taking this step of faith, are more wonderful and plentiful than could be detailed in a single volume. But receiving God's wonderful gift of eternal life, as made possible by Christ, is the greatest "That's God" event one can ever experience. For me, it took place as a child, under the simple Bible teaching of Dr. Raymond Hancock. Thus began a long series of "That's God" experiences in my life.

In Lamentations 3:23, Jeremiah wrote "His mercies are new every morning..." How true! Every day is a new adventure, in the life of the one who loves and serves God. So, not only have Debbie and I seen God's providence through the stories related in this book, (as well as the many not mentioned here); but each new day is pregnant with possibilities of more and more personal encounters with the God Who loves and cares for us so personally. Therefore, the journey continues. I, for one, want to enjoy the journey, as well as the destination. My hope and prayer is that you can say the same. But as you do, don't overlook those moments when God interrupts, intersects, interjects, or intervenes in your life, demonstrating His sweet providence to you. I love the saying that goes something like, "Life is not measured by the number of moments we're given, or the number of breaths we take; but by those moments which take our breath away. May your own "That's God" moments be rich and plentiful.